KNOW YOURSELF

PURPOSE & MEANING OF LIFE AND LAWS OF SUCCESS

DR S K SACHAN | PH. D.

ISBN 979-888629145-2

This book is dedicated to my family and friends.

It's also dedicated to my Grandparents, Father, and other loved ones who have passed away. They have always provided me with the ability to walk the path of righteousness and to proceed with duty, commitment, and dedication. Unless we have forgotten about them, our dead are never truly dead. They are to be commended.

Contents

Preface

It gives me immense pleasure to share this book with you. The book is designed to be straightforward but comprehensive. The title of the book "KNOW YOURSELF - PURPOSE & MEANING OF LIFE and LAWS OF SUCCESS "is of common concern to everyone in our day today life and it covers all aspects of the Human life from being among family members and in community, in colleges, at work, in workplaces, in the military, after military as a veteran, in aging and retirement.

The underlying concern of this piece of writing is to encourage thought and reflection – more importantly for you the readers to think about yourself, your relationship to the world, and those other selves you encounter daily.

The major goal of this book is to explain concepts in a clear and succinct manner that will benefit the readers. The fundamental notions have been established in a systematic and steady manner.

Acknowledgements

I wish to personally thank the people for their contributions to my inspiration and knowledge and other help in creating this book.

I'd like to express my gratitude to my parents, my own family, relatives, colleagues and friends, without whom none of this would have been possible.

After thanking my family for their endless support, I would like to thank a few more people here. I am really grateful to my school teachers, professors, senior Officers in military service, seniors/colleagues in Govt. service and society at large for their support, suggestions, guidance, motivation and reviews throughout my life including college days and service period for leading a dutiful, disciplined, dedicated and purposeful life, without whom this would not have been possible.

These people were always present to help me in learning new things whenever I needed them. Working with these people was a steep learning curve for me as they did not only polish my life skills but also gave me an insight into the dimensions of the livings in this real world.

Last but not the least; I thank from core of my heart all philosophers, writers, bloggers, various websites on Internet media, TEDx talks on You Tube Channels, Online course through Coursera Education, whose references have been used in this manuscript.

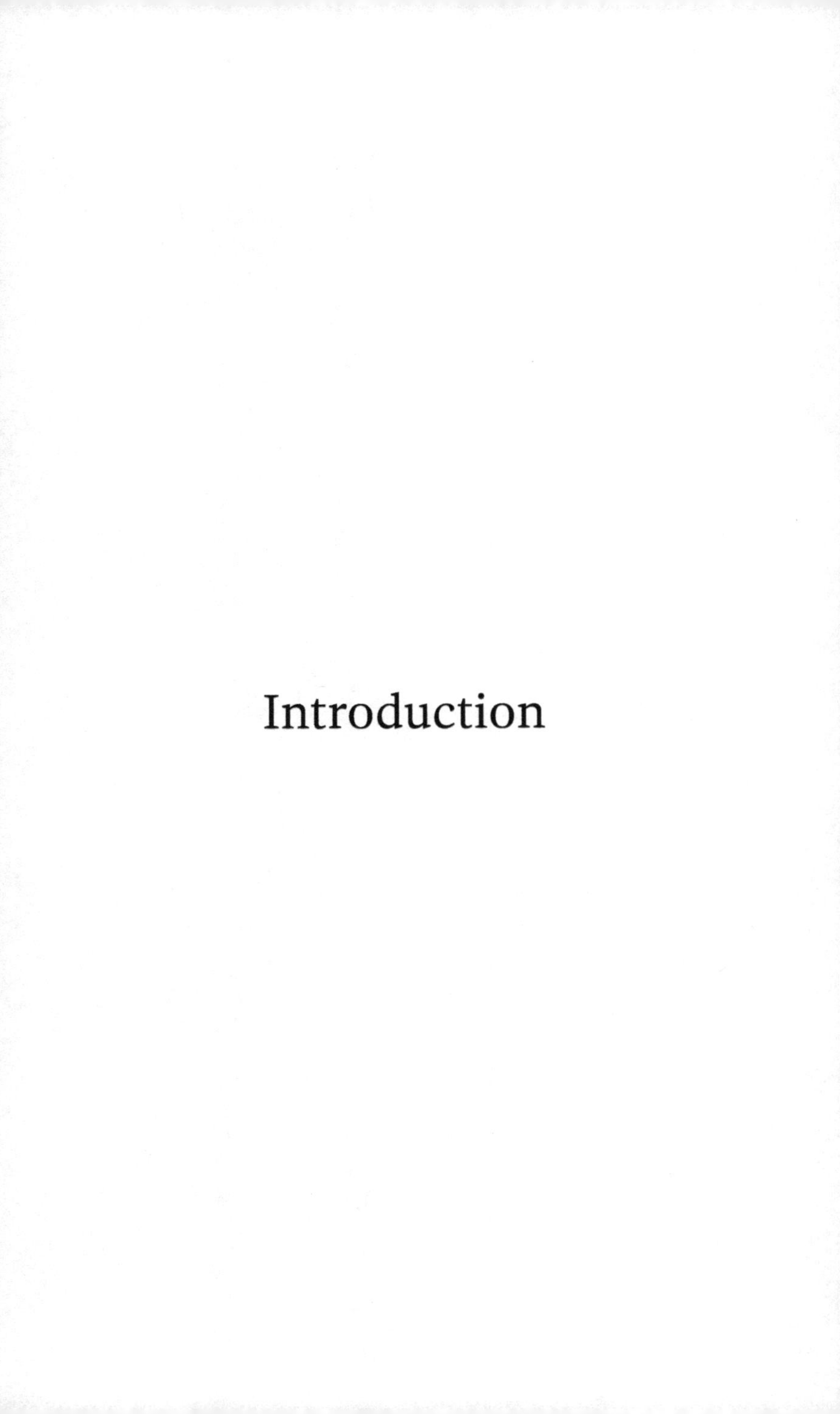

Introduction

INTRODUCTION

The title of the book, "KNOW YOURSELF - PURPOSE & MEANING OF LIFE and LAWS OF SUCCESS "is of common concern to everyone in our day today life and it covers all aspects of the Human life from being in colleges, at work, in workplaces, in the military, after military as a veteran, in aging and retirement, among family members and in community.

The underlying concern of this piece of writing is to encourage thought and reflection – more importantly for you the readers to think about yourself, your relationship to the world, and those other selves you encounter daily. A lot of material is available on the subject at different places especially philosophical books (Western and Indian), journals, blogs, internet media etc. and most of you like youngsters, student, elders and educationists might already be aware of most of the things enumerated here but still you can have a look once again and refresh your memories. If you already have found out the purpose and understood the meaning of life and you are also aware of various laws of success in life, you can transform your life and still find a way further for betterment of it. Those who are not yet aware of it can also find a way out and shape their life, existence accordingly after reading it.

I attempted to collect the subject material from several sources and compiled into a succinct format. I am grateful to all of the authors, columnists, philosophical thinkers, existentialists (Existentialism, a philosophical theory or approach which emphasizes the existence of the individual person as a free and responsible agent determining their own development through acts of the will) and other contributors, whose words/works influenced me to bring the topic together in one place for the benefit of everyone who reads this piece of writing. I have also taken into a brief account on the views of existentialists, I mentioned in my earlier book "Human Liberty and responsibility in existentialism: Theistic and Atheistic existentialists" based on my thesis submitted for my Ph.D degree.

Now, let us begin with the basic question that who thought of this, who founded the idea, how to find purpose in life, meaning of life and make yourself a better person, and what are the various ways helpful in finding the purpose in life. What are the laws of success which can really help you to lead a very happy, healthy, peaceful and prosperous life, living in a very congenial atmosphere in this very world? It is a matter of general belief that there is only this single life which has to be lived with utmost sincerity. Since, it is hard for me to believe that there is another world and there is another life after this very life; as a result, personally, I do not believe in any Avatar, incarnation, or rebirth after this very life or existence which has come to an end. Death is the end of life and nothing can be retrieved out of it once life ceases to exist. By saying this, I do not wish to play with the sentiments of others who believe in all these things as said above. Everyone has their own life, beliefs, understanding, faith, and religion to practice, among many other things not stated here. The author respects everyone's existing religious beliefs. Let us now return to the purpose and meaning of life, as well as the laws of success, if we practice wisely might bring a radical change in the life and living of human beings altogether.

So, now in the next chapter, let's start with the purpose and meaning of life.

What is a purpose and meaning of life?

CHAPTER TWO

WHAT IS A PURPOSE AND MEANING OF LIFE?

The "meaning of life" has been debated since the dawn of time, and it is one of the most fundamental and ultimate concerns that has enthralled humanity's best minds for ages. According to Evelyn Marinoff [1], a Canadian writer/researcher who writes about the psychology behind confidence, happiness, and well-being; "Living a meaningful life appears to be the ultimate goal". Many questions on a purpose and meaning of life can be raised and the answers to these question, as diverse as they are, can be traced all the way back to the beginning of time—to our existence, the reasons why people were "made," our goal for self-improvement, and, of course, religion.

There are many different perspectives on what the "good life" entails, what makes us happy and content, and how we might achieve this coveted state.

If you ask a scientist—say, a physicist and a biologist—about the meaning of life, they will most likely tell you about the Big Bang, the origins of the cosmos, and the evolution of the species to where we are now.

But evolution isn't what actually motivates us to keep living and persevering in the face of adversity, is it? There's a lot more to it than that. It is our thoughts, our feeling of self-awareness, our ambitions, dreams, and objectives that make us human.

So, when pondering your reasons for existence, consider your values, advancement, community, family, and, yes, reproduction.

First and foremost, let's see what other writers have to say about the subject. Evelyn Marinoff has discovered the purpose of life within the following headings:

1. Historical Perspectives on Living with Meaning
2. How to Find Your Life's Purpose
3. How to Live a Meaningful Life
4. What Gives Your Life Meaning?
5. More Thoughts on the Meaning of Life

Historical Perspectives on Living with Meaning

Before we unpack these elements of meaning, let's take a step back and see what wise men through history believed a purpose of life to be.

The Greeks

The ancient Greeks believed in the concept of *eudemonia,* which translates as "happiness" or "welfare." All the great Greek philosophers—Socrates, Plato, Aristotle—believed that the good life means to live in a state of eudemonia.

The interpretations of what it means vary. Some used to think that purpose can be found in acquiring virtues (as self-control, courage, wisdom). [1] (A)

Aristotle, for instance, believed that eudemonia required not only a good character, but taking actions and achieving excellence. Epicurus—another prominent Greek—understood the good life as one of pleasure and freedom from pain and suffering.

Cynicism (Pessimism)

The famous Greek school of thought believed that the meaning of life is living a life of Virtue that agrees with Nature. The happy life is the simple one, they taught—free from possessions, rejecting the desires for wealth, possessions, fame, or sex. Rather, people should undergo rigorous training and live in way that is most natural to them. [2]

Stoicism

Stoicism is a Hellenistic philosophy school founded in Athens in the early third century BC by Zeno of Citium. It is a personal eudemonic virtue ethics philosophy inspired by its logic and perspectives on the natural world, arguing that virtue practice is both essential and sufficient for achieving eudemonia - thriving - through living an ethical life. The Stoics identified a life devoted practicing the cardinal virtues and living in harmony with nature as the way to eudemonia.

The Stoics are especially known for teaching that "virtue is the only good" for human beings, and those external things—such as health, wealth, and pleasure—are not good or bad in themselves (adiaphora, a Greek word which means "indifferent"), but have value as "material for virtue to act upon". Alongside Aristotelian ethics, the Stoic tradition forms one of the major founding approaches to virtue ethics. The Stoics also held that certain destructive emotions resulted from errors of judgment, and they believed people should aim to maintain a will (called prohairesis, a Greek word which means "moral character", "volition", "choice", "intention", or "moral choice") that is "in accordance with nature". Because of this, the Stoics thought the best indication of an individual's philosophy was not what a person said but how a person behaved. To live a good life, one had to understand the rules of the natural order since they thought everything was rooted in nature.

Theism

Theists believed in the presence of a deity, or God, who was responsible for the creation of the cosmos. Our lives' purpose is thus connected with God's goal in creating the universe, and it is God who gives meaning, purpose, and values to our existence. This has to do with current religious studies and how and why we look for meaning outside of what we can see or understand.

Because the topic is more closely tied to philosophy than any other discipline that can answer these concerns, and because philosophers can only answer them in a more thorough fashion, it would be my endeavour to discuss it, given the topic's complexity.

Existentialism

Existentialism is an issue that has arisen of contemporary philosophy. It originated in Denmark, developed in Germany and matured in France. This philosophy repudiates all those philosophical principles who have accepted as a main subject of philosophical thinking, the external world and not the man. Existentialists' center of thinking is man and they consider existent human being as their subject of thinking in this world. Though all existentialists' philosophers are not one on the subject but they agree to some extent while discussing human existence that (1) man is free (2) and that man is responsible for himself.

As a movement of thought, existentialism reaches back for its origin into the 19th century to the Danish Theologian Soren Aabye Kierkegaard, and to the strange German genius Friedrich Wilhelm Nietzsche but it crystallized out in the forties and fifties of this century in France. There are various reasons why existentialism coming from Germany where Karl Jaspers and Martin Heidegger developed it, as did JP Sartre and Gabriel Marcel in France appealed to such a wide stratum of intellectuals. [3]

As said, Existentialism is a philosophy that began to emerge in the early eighteen hundreds. It is difficult to define or categorize because it has no single organized expression. It is actually a philosophical stance that emerged out of the attempt to find meaning in life without acknowledging the existence of God.

While there is no singular existentialist perspective, the philosophy is defined by specific ideas. Existentialists' writings are frequently on existence, change, freedom, and self-awareness. Everything is subjective, and "being" comes before "doing," according to the main doctrine that binds them all together.

Existentialism is atheistic since it is based on a naturalistic worldview. There is, however, a secular and a religious version. Even the religious variety, however, is agnostic. Essentially, it simply takes religious jargon and redefines it to reflect Existentialist views.

Secular Existentialism

The secular variant of Existentialism is by far the most common. It is devoid of any religious overtones. Martin

Heidegger, Karl Jaspers, and Jean-Paul Sartre are among the members of this group. The following are some of the primary themes.

Being is divided into three categories: 1) concern, 2) existence, and 3) moods. The essence of a human being is his existence.

Individuals have the freedom to choose several types of "being" for themselves.

Angst Anxiety, dreads, hopelessness, and fear of the future are all terms used to describe angst. It is the feeling of fear that an individual feels when he realizes that his very existence is at jeopardy. The void left by a sense of hopelessness must be filled by the individual's freely chosen choices.

Death - There is no existence before or after death ("We didn't exist before we were born. When we die, we return to that state). The person, who recognizes this fact, freely accepts the inevitability of death and seeks nothing beyond this life. At that point he becomes free to choose his own existence and is no longer bound by fear.

Absurdity - Life is absurd. If life is to have any meaning at all, the individual must create that meaning for himself.

Autonomy - God does not exist. An individual must create his own values and way of living and can't blame anyone else for the outcome.

Freedom - There is no outside entity or authority to define man. He must define himself and has absolute freedom to do so.

Existence Before Essence - Man, by his own choices, defines his character, his essence and the person he is becoming. His choices determine his make-up. Man exists, and from that existence he creates his own essence.

Fulfillment - Man makes his own fulfillment. He can create whatever he likes, and in so doing will determine for himself what is fulfilling.

Forlornness (depression) - This is a state that people find themselves in when they understand that they are alone and must determine their own being.

Religious Existentialism

Religious existentialists have the same basic concept of reality as their secular counterparts.

In their explanations, they are simply willing to use the word "God" and other Christian terminology. When reading these authors, keep in mind that they redefine religious terms to convey godless existential philosophy. The concept of subjectivity is important to everything in existential thought, as it is to all existential thought. God and grace are two fundamental religious terms that have been modified to symbolize Existentialist philosophy.

God, according to religious Existentialists, is "the root of one's being," "the ground of all being," or "one's ultimate concern." This is not a personal God, but rather the meaning that emerges from a person's innermost concern (angst).

Grace is regarded as both universal and personal. It circulates back and forth between individuals. During a crisis, it is a person's subjective sensation of acceptance.

Karl Barth, Paul Tillich, Rudolph Boltzmann, Soren Kierkegaard, and Gabriel Marcel are among the most renowned members of this faction.

Basic Beliefs and Practices

There are six common themes that are generally found in Existentialist writings.

1. **Experience is the basis of understanding** - Existentialist philosophy arises from "existential"

experience – that which is based on observable or experimental evidence. This experience is unique to each person.

2. **Existence is the most important thing to try and understand** - While it is the most important thing to understand, it is often quite difficult to grasp what is meant by the word existence. Essentially, it is understood to be that which consciously exists. In their definition of the term, man is alone possesses existence.

3. **Existence precedes essence** - A thing must be aware of itself in order to exist in the way that Existentialists speak of it.

4. **Man is pure subjectivity and is not part of a transcendent life process** - There is no transcendent being who gives meaning to man's existence. Man creates meaning on his own by living life and by personally interpreting his own subjective life experience.

5. **There is interdependence between man and his world** - An individual is incomplete in and of himself. Man's nature ties him absolutely to the world and to other people.

6. **Intellectual knowledge is of low value** - All existentialists deny any distinction between subject and object. Because of that, intellectual knowledge is seen to have little value. True knowledge is not achieved by the intellect, but through subjectively experiencing reality.

Essential Beliefs

God

The concept of God is not even considered by secular existentialists. According to religious existentialists, God is just the meaning that emerges from a person's primary concern in life. In essence, there is a complete denial of any transcendent existence.

Man

The essence of a human being is the fact that he exists at all. A person's essence can be defined in a variety of ways, and each person must pick his or her own identity.

Salvation

The subjective sense of acceptance that one feels amid a crisis is referred to as salvation. Fulfillment happens when a person pushes beyond his or her feelings of despondency and anxiety and embraces the true fact of existence (that life is pointless).

Faith Foundation

1. What is the nature of material reality and
2. What is the most fundamental reality? (Ultimate reality)

Matter is the only thing that exists, and it is everlasting, evolving, and the outcome of natural principles that operate indefinitely.

3. What is the definition of a human being? (Humanity)

Humans are nothing more than sophisticated biological machinery. They are the consequence of billions of years of evolutionary processes at work. The essence of a human being is his consciousness of his own existence. A person has the freedom to choose several types of "being" for himself.

4. What happens to a person once they pass away? (Death) When a person dies, their particular life form just vanishes.

5. How is it even possible to know anything? (Knowledge)

Knowledge is only a byproduct of a high level of evolution in the human animal.

6. How do we know what is correct and what is incorrect? (Morality)

No theory of morality can be said to have a transcendent reason. Individuals or social groups decide what is right and wrong in order to determine what is best for society's survival and comfort.

7. What does it mean to be a part of human history? (History)

History has no significance. It's merely a chronological sequence of events that moves from the past to the future.

Authority

There is no recognized scripture, but there are a number of writers who propose various forms of existentialism.

Evidence for the Authority

Since existentialism is based entirely on the ideas of individual thinkers, there is nothing to give it any validation except for the individuals, themselves, who assert it. There is no external or empirical evidence to back up their claims. According to this 20th century philosophy, supported by famous minds such as Soren Kierkegaard, Fyodor Dostoevsky, Jean-Paul Sartre, and Friedrich Nietzsche, all human beings have free will. It's believed that each person gives meaning to their own life, not the society or religion. Therefore, everyone's purpose is unique and subjective to their circumstances and understanding. [4]

Simply put, your life's meaning is what you decide it to be.

What Creates Meaning to Your Life?

Based on the foregoing brief historical tour, it appears that the interpretation of what gives our existence value and purpose changes depending on the historical period and school of thought.

However, there are some unmistakable similarities and repeating themes. Something higher than ourselves develops as our reason for existing, such as serving God's will or contributing to society. It's all nuanced at the same time because it's filtered through our particular prisms.

Still, there are a few basic types of items that could be ideal candidates for meaning-creators in our lives:

Social

As human beings are social creatures, we have an innate need to connect to others, to be part of a group, to sense that we belong, and that we have someone who cares about us.

According to the longest study on happiness and life satisfaction [5], which spanned over 75 years, the good life lies in the quality of our relationships. "Time with others," Prof. Waldinger, who led the research tells us, "Protects us from the bruises of life's ups and downs."

But it's not only our friendships that make life worth living. It's our families, children, and siblings. It's all the people who we feel love and affection for and who, in turn, give us theirs.

Achievement

Although tying our worth solely to the outcome of our endeavors can create an unstable sense of self-esteem, we still want the net of our successes to outnumber that of our failings. We want to sense that we are moving forward, progressing, and realizing our goals.

Studies have found that achievements bring greater meaning to our everyday lives. [6]

And it won't be the allure of the spotlight or the yearning for plaudits that will justify our existence. What matters is that our efforts are recognized, that we are appreciated, and that we are acknowledged. To put it another way, we want our activities to matter and have an impact.

Competence, Knowledge and Expertise

These purpose-drivers are closely linked to the concept of achievement.

Konrad Lorenz [7], the Austrian Nobel Prize winner, best known for his principle of attachment, once said:

"Life itself is a process of acquiring knowledge."

Becoming the best at what we do is a large part of the self-improvement movement today. It's perhaps most famously expressed in the Japanese notions of *kaizen* and *shokunin*. Kaizen is the process of continuous improvement—through learning and gaining expertise, to better ourselves as a way of life.

Shokunin means craftsman. And it's about taking pride in what we do and in ourselves. It's the drive to become better—personally and professionally.

How to Craft Your Own Purpose in Life

However, there are many more colours and interpretations of a well-lived life than the three criteria stated above.

Here are some more suggestions for finding your own sense of purpose and fulfillment.

1. Be Aware of What Makes You Happy

This encompasses your interests, as well as your drive to interact with others, read, write, travel, and keep in shape. Even if these activities do not provide you with the One Meaning of your Life, they have the ability to make you pleased and joyful.

They are joyous spurs. You might think of them as mini-meanings that, over time, may help you achieve your larger goals and purposes.

But they'll still give you something to look forward to today, a reason to get out of bed in the morning.

2. **Reproduction**

Evolutionary biology reveals the most fundamental reason for our existence as humans: to assure the survival of human life for the foreseeable future. That is, meaning is determined by our kin's survival and continuation.

In this line, when individuals discuss what makes life worth living, having children and a family is frequently at or near the top of the list. This is similar to our basic urge to belong and have someone with whom we can share our accomplishments.

3. **Desire to Leave a Mark in the World**

With the understanding of our lives' transience comes a natural urge to produce something worthwhile to leave behind.

We all have the ability to have an impact on the lives of others. You can start small—whatever it is that matters to you—and build from there.

If you like animals, for example, you can adopt a puppy and offer it a better life. You can also help the environment by volunteering at a local food bank or beginning to sort your rubbish.

"We can do no large things, but modest things with tremendous love," Mother Teresa famously stated.

Caring is important to living a meaningful life.

Howto Lead a Meaningful Life

1. Be Compassionate and Care About Yourself

According to research by the British National Health Service in 2014, there are five steps we can take to lead more meaningful lives: [8]

Connect with community and family

Physical exercise

Lifelong learning

Giving to others

Mindfulness of the world around you

What these recommendations imply is that what brings sunshine into our lives is finding the ways to care about ourselves and to do what makes us feel good.

There is barely a need to convince you of the benefits of giving and meditation—these are well established—to both our physical and mental health.

Being kind, compassionate, and helping others are, indeed, the winning behaviors to increased longevity and decreased stressed and depression so that we can also experience life in all its colorfulness.

2. Make Yourself Useful

According to Darius Foroux, a famous entrepreneur, author, and influencer, the meaning of life is not to seek happiness, but to make ourselves useful [9].

"It comes down to this—what are you DOING that's making a difference?"

Rather than seeking happiness and meaning through the material things, we must engage in acts of usefulness—to help and make others happy, to create something.

"The last thing I want is to be on my deathbed and realize there's zero evidence that I ever existed."

3. Connect With the World

Another influencer, Alain de Botton, the founder of the famous blog "The School of Life", believes that the meaning of life comes down to three activities: [10]

Communication

Understanding

Service

"Some of our most meaningful moments are to do with instances of connection," he writes, be it to a person, song, or a book, for instance. It takes us out of our isolation. Understanding is our ability to make sense of the world, and service is to work on improving others' lives.

4. Use the PURE Model

Finally, Peter Wong—a Canadian existential psychologist has proposed a model known as PURE for individuals to discover meaning in their lives: [11]

P: **Purpose** and having worthy goals.

U: **Understating**—of who we are and of the world around us.

R: We have sole **responsibility** to choose the life we want and to own our actions and their consequences.

E: **Evaluation,** to ensure we are on track with our goals.

There are many avenues you can explore that will bring you a sense of purpose. It's true that you may sometimes feel that your actions are just a drop in the ocean, that you are too small to make a difference.

But it's not true.

Meaning is about bringing out the best in you, about doing well by yourself and others.

As corny as it may sound, if we all commit to the objective of bettering ourselves and the world we live in, a single drop can turn into a wave.

Summarizing Everything

The search for meaning in our lives is possibly the most powerful motivator for all we do. It's the reason behind everything. And there isn't a straightforward solution to the question.

Creating your own tribe, wanting to become a better version of yourself, helping and serving others, and setting objectives and attempting to attain them are some of the most notable ways to build your purpose.

The fact that purpose is such a broad term makes it difficult to pin down exactly what it entails. It can be construed in a variety of ways by each of us.

Perhaps, in the end, **there is no one and only meaning in life.** Perhaps a better way to view our purpose and existence is more as a mosaic. Each experience, each facet in our lives—family, friends, achievements, recognition—constitutes a piece. You have to look at it in its totality to be able to say if you are happy with the picture you yourself have painted.

Or, perhaps, it is as Viktor Frankl said:

"The meaning of life is to give life meaning."

And each of us has the freedom to decide on what when and how life is meaningful.

Who was the founder of the idea of purpose in life?

As far back as the fourth century BC, Aristotle was pondering life's purpose and developing his theory of teleology, or the idea that everything in life has purpose. In today's fast-paced, technology-filled world where we are being pulled in many directions at once, finding your purpose seems more important than ever.

How to find your purpose in Your Life?

It's what life is all about: discovering your mission and living it out. What motivates you, what gets you out of bed in the morning, and what gives you energy is your mission. If you only do one thing with your life, seek your purpose with all your heart to enjoy the rewards of a meaningful existence!

Why do I have no sense of purpose in my life?

When people feel as if they have no sense of direction or purpose in their lives, it's because they don't know what matters to them or what their values are. And if you don't know what your values are, you're essentially adopting other people's values and prioritizing other people's goals rather than your own.

Different Ways to Find Your Purpose in Life

Having a meaningful, long-term objective is beneficial to your health. Here's where you can look for one.

Do you ever question why you're even here? You know, like how to find your life's meaning or purpose? Why are you on this earth in the first place?

These are perhaps the most subtle, yet significant, questions people ask themselves on a daily basis, and I'm sure there are as many varied answers as there are people asking them.

This is why, rather than asking yourself why you are here and what you should be doing, let us start by making your experiences the answers to your questions and reintroducing some meaning and get-up-and-go into your life.

1. Learn the Lesson on Happiness

You've probably heard it before, but happiness is a decision. Yes, and fortunately, anyone can practice it because the truth is that you can actually override what you were taught, which was to play along with the rest of the world and become agitated or sad because things aren't ideal.

Okay, I'm not saying you should continuously wear a delusional smile (people would think you're insane), but you should keep calm and joyful when dealing with problems that require your attention.

2. Follow Your Gifts and Talents

Discovering your strengths and talents can help you find your purpose and add meaning to your life. Here are some questions to assist you figure out what underlying talents and gifts you have:

What is it that you are naturally good at?

When do you think you're at your best?

So, what are you doing or going through right now?

In what ways do you like assisting others?

3. Make Great Connections

Spend time with people that make your life better and lift you up. This might include everyone from friends to co-workers.

Spend less time with folks who sap your energy or give you bad vibes all the time. "You are the average of the five individuals you spend the most time with," Jim Rohn says.

Begin to pay attention to how you feel while you're in the company of people. (You should be in a pleasant mood.)

4. Goal Setting

If you want your life to have meaning, you must make a plan. You don't have to sit down for five hours every Monday to create goals for the rest of the week that you'll almost certainly fail to meet—please doesn't do this to yourself!

Have goals, nevertheless, and a strategy for reaching them. It shouldn't be something you despise doing, but rather have a list of accomplishments you'd like to see in your life and make a plan to achieve them by writing them down. Then, most importantly, do something about it.

Learn how to reclaim your optimism and get your life back on track by following these simple steps to developing a positive and powerful mentality.

Are you looking for some motivation to set goals?

5. Help Others

Giving back to others makes you feel good, makes you feel worthy, and gives you a feeling of purpose. Giving to others in the form of time, money, or any other form of assistance is a surefire method to give oneself meaning in life.

So, here's the question: Do you know anyone who could be able to assist you in the future?

6. Do Something Different

Why not visit a museum, have lunch at a posh hotel in your hometown, or spend the day pampering yourself at home? You're probably so engrossed in your daily routine that you believe you don't have time for it.

Doing something unusual interrupts the pattern of 'doing' life and allows you to take a break from the routine and realize you're losing out on some of life's most meaningful moments.

7. Quit Watching TV/Smartphone

Seriously, I challenge you to go a week without watching TV or using your phone, especially if you find it difficult to live without the news. You'll notice a difference in your life, and you'll begin to understand how seductive the TV/Smartphone, as well as the entire negative it portrays.

Do you want to rediscover the significance in your life? Then switch off the TV/phone and do something worthwhile with your time. Simple!

8. Do something you've always wanted to do

Step1. Identify your 'thing'.

Step2. Go do it.

If this is an impossible two-step process for you right now, then start working towards, saving, learning or doing whatever it will take to make it happen. But make your first step!

9. Find Your Purpose

Finding your purpose, in my opinion, is one of the most liberating things you can do in life. This will provide you with all of the significance you need in your life. It's what life is all about: discovering your mission and living it out.

How purpose organizes our life?

HOW PURPOSE ORGANIZES OUR LIFE?

Apart from the above discussion of finding purpose and meaning in life in Chapter 2, I'd also like to quote a lecture delivered by Dr. Victor Strecher [1] of the University of Michigan's School of Public Health through [Audio, Video, and Class Room on-line lecture] based on his book "Life on Purpose," which has influenced me the most while taking a certification course on "Finding a Purpose and Meaning in Life: Living on What Matters Most" at the University of Michigan. During his presentation via audio, video, and Class Room on-line lectures, he quoted many existentialist philosophers who were part of my Ph.D thesis on "Human Liberty and Responsibility in Existentialism". He has explained the concept taking help of various activities, exercises and also conducted numerous scientific researches with the MRI technology to determine the meaning and purpose of life by measuring blood flow in the ventral medial prefrontal cortex (*The ventral medial prefrontal is located in the frontal lobe at the bottom of the*

cerebral hemispheres and is implicated in the processing of risk and fear, as it is critical in the regulation of amygdala activity in humans. It also plays a role in the inhibition of emotional responses, and in the process of decision making and self control) and amygdala *(The amygdala is a small structure located in the temporal lobes of the brain. It plays an important role in emotion and memory. There are two amygdalae in the brain. One is in the right hemisphere and other is in the left hemisphere. The amygdala is part of the limbic system).* It would be a disservice to everyone if I did not provide such elements in this book.

So, welcome to purposeful living, where doing what matters most transforms everything. We will discuss what it means to have a purpose & meaning in life and how purpose organizes our lives from both a philosophical and scientific standpoint. We will also discuss how purpose affects our lives into the real world and know about how purpose works in very different situations ranging from being in college (Author completed Bachelor of Science (Biology), Bachelor of Education, Masters of Arts in Political Science, English literature, philosophy and Ph.D in philosophy), to being at work (Author served Indian Ordnance Factories under Govt. of India), being in the military (Author served Indian Air Force), growing older and retirement (now, Author is an Air Veteran/pensioner), and many other situations in real life like family and community. So let's start out with the general principles of this subject. First, we're going to be using a lot of science, but we're also going to be talking about philosophy. Initially, we're going to cover a fair amount of philosophy. Why do we cover all this philosophy, including some ancient philosophy? Simple, because, Philosophy, the word "philosophy" originated from the Greek word φιλοσοφία (philosophia). "Philo" means to love and "Sophia" means wisdom. Literally, philosophy means love of wisdom. Philosophy actually frames our science in this case. Philosophy is also known to be the science of sciences. And that is the reason that even today all Doctoral degree i.e. Ph.D in any subject is awarded as Doctor of Philosophy i.e. Ph.D in Science, Math's, Physics and Chemistry etc. So it's really important to have some depth of the philosophy and some amazing thinking about that, and what led to how we think about the science now. Apart from that, it should be our endeavour and all the way we should strive to make the world a better place to live. I really believe that if you begin to establish a better purpose in your life, and if you assist others in doing the same, we will live in a better world. To be honest, our world is losing its meaning, and we all to be concerned about losing our purpose concerning various issues like climate change, pollution (especially air and water), and various fatal diseases such as covid-19; Corona and its various variants, to name a few like Delta and Omicron, which recently claimed the lives of millions and still claiming, or about many other things in the world, and I rightly believe that we need to begin building greater purpose more significance in the globe for making life and living of each inhabitant better.

Self-affirmation is a crucial and closely related concept to purpose and being purposeful, because you might have a goal but not be purposeful. It's difficult to be purposeful without having a purpose; therefore we'll look at some of the key components of purpose that are related to philosophical topics, the background required framing out the science of purpose, as well as attempting to organize these ideas in a logical manner. So, first and foremost, what is the purpose of life? The purpose of life is a central self-organizing life aim. And there are two sub components of this. By central self-organizing life aim, it's a predominant theme of a person's self. And it also motivates intention to dedicate resources in a particular direction and toward particular goals.

Self-analysis is a very meaningful habit which helps in testing one-self in other words, forces one to verify one's personality. It helps in finding flaws in one-self and exceptions one has in his life. When one tries to find one's mistakes, this has two benefits. First, one can find drawbacks in one-self and try to remove them and this helps one's mind to think about one-self. Secondly, this saves most of the time that one has wasted in finding other's mistakes. All-time one will be busy thinking about oneself and ultimately will have no time to think about others. So Self-analysis helps in evolving one's mindset; and helps not only in improving personality but also in finding purpose in life.

Let's start with the first important point, which states that it is a major theme in a person's life. This pertains to the fact that it is important and a life goal. So, who are you? Isn't that what we're actually asking? What is your life's central theme? What are you, who are you? Those are extremely essential considerations. I'd want to start with the concept of a theme. What exactly do you mean by theme? Here's what I mean by theme: we can have custom-made theme colours. We've recently moved into a new home and want to paint it a certain colour scheme. Well, what types of thematic colours you want, the painter would ask what kinds of thematic colours do you want? And you chose a single colour from millions of colours available as per your likings. In the end, when the work is finished, it becomes evident how the constraint of a single taste governed and formed everything large and small. Friedrich Nietzsche was a philosopher in the mid to late 1800s, very influential to the whole existentialist philosophy movement. And this is an interesting thing; he says basically, there's a single taste or a single theme that starts governing other things. And when he says the work is finished, he's really talking about your purpose.

So we're debating, "Who am I?" What am I all about? In order to find out the very answer to the question, Dr Victor Strecher gives a short activity to help us figure out who we are. He says, when you're at your best, you're thinking about yourself. So he believes that we all have times when we feel at our best and are our best selves, and then there are times when we aren't. He believes that we all have those moments, and there are some times or methods we can see ourselves at our finest a little more frequently. One of the benefits of having a purpose is that it motivates you to be your best self more often. So that's a fantastic way to start thinking about who you are and what's important to you. So here is a bunch of different ways of being your best self. Do you love, for example? Are you kind? Are you healthy? Are you funny? Think about what you're like when you're at your best. Are you super active? Are you connected? Are you empathetic? Are you courageous? Let's go through a list of a couple of other best self characteristics. Are you grateful? Are you dependable? Are you happy? Are you calm, resilient? Are you energized or hardworking, engaged? Are you community-minded? Are you caring when you're at your best self? Are you balanced when you're at your best? Are you supportive or generous, or creative or patient? Are you growing or optimistic? Are you mindful? All of these things relate to what you might be when you're at your best. If you had to pick two of these, or three or so, what would you pick? What are you like when you're at your best? This often becomes the beginning point for asking, who am I? Because we don't want you to be who you are when you're at your worst, we want you to be who are you when you're at your best, because that's what your real self, your aspiration self could be. So I might pick, "Oh, when I'm at my best, I'm calm, and I'm resilient." So it's clear now that how purpose in life is a central self-organizing life aim and who am I, what is my central theme, what is my character?

The second is really important in that it's looking at motivating intention to dedicate resources which means, your time, about your energy, maybe about your money or other things. It's basically devoting what you have to give to particular directions and toward particular goals. One thing that a purpose in life does is help you focus on the things that matter most in your life. So that you're not so spread out across so many different things that your energy and your time is just being devoted to way too many things, and you have no focus. So a purpose in life reduces conflict by building focus for your efforts.

The second important point is really asking this question [2]: what are the directions in my life, what are the goals in my life, and very importantly, what do I value in my life? How do we find out what we value? That process, by the way, is called self-affirmation. So when we're affirming our self, we're starting to reflect on personally relevant values. This is a really key and much related concept to purpose in life. So just think about this like, what do I value? How do I even find out? Well, maybe you want to even start with your Smartphone. What's on the wallpaper of my Smartphone? This is my father. He has been on the wallpaper of my Smartphone for a while because he was 73 years old, and I loved him a lot, and he had developed severe ILD, and it was just a wonderful experience being able to spend some time with him, some really high value, and high quality time with him. So your father might be on your Smartphone or your mother. There could be somebody who you've lost.

In order to find out what you value, Dr Victor Strecher gives a little exercise comprising seven questions to have you think about, first of all, **what matters most in your life?** What are things that are most important in your life? Another question is **who relies on you?** Do you have kids who rely on you? Do you have parents who rely on you? Do you have siblings who rely on you? How about friends? Do you have a dog or a cat that relies on you? So do you have people who rely on you? Because those people become super important, I hope they're super important to you because they rely on you. And then another question is **who inspires you?** And this could be a person who is alive or a person who is no more. Could be Aristotle inspires you, or Mahatma Gandhi inspires you. But it also could be your mother or your father, could be a brother or sister. It could be a friend or some public figure that inspires you. So think about who inspires you when you're thinking about what you value the most in your life. Again, we're trying to focus on the things that are most important in your life. Another might be **what causes do you care about?** So think about now, whether it's some political cause or an environmental cause or maybe a local cause, maybe it's a cause related to the arts. So what are some causes that you care about? **What are you grateful for?** Who are the people that you're grateful for? What's the situation that you might be grateful for? Are you grateful for living where you are, for example? Another is **what gets you out of bed in the morning?** When you're waking up, you might just want to sleep in because you have nothing that gets you out of bed. But when you are thinking about, I have to get up and do this, what is that? Is that an important thing to you? Is it something that you value? What gets you out of bed? And finally, **how do you want to be remembered?** This is a really important one in Psychology, we call this mortality salience. Now just think about that in terms of life. Let's say there was no death. Let's say we lived forever. How would we live our lives? Would we live our lives differently if we live forever than if we lived a finite period of time? Well, I think the answer is pretty obvious. If we lived forever we would just kind of assumed that eventually something would get done with that person who's having a hard time. If we could live forever maybe we would just not really worry about every individual day being important, every individual minute. You always say you're going to die every single day and yet you come home alive. And he might say well, I do that so that I'll live a bigger life today. So I appreciate the day that I was alive today, and I'm going to put everything I possibly have into that day. That is purposeful living, which is living a big life. That's why thinking about your death oddly enough creates more life. So, for example, Steve Jobs was dying of pancreatic cancer when he gave the commencement address in 2005 to the Stanford graduating class. And this is what he said. Imagine how much he must have shocked the graduating students at Stanford, who had everything ahead of them, you would think. And he said death is very likely the single best invention of life. It's life's change agent. Can you imagine being a student at that time and he's talking all about death and how important death is? Well, he understood that because he knew he is going to die pretty soon, and he started realizing how valuable life was, every single day. People who are in hospital for example, start changing their life, in the way that they think. They say man; I wish I had lived my life the way I am right now, appreciating every single minute, every single hour. I wish I had done that during the regular part of my life. So this is such an important thing to be thinking about your death.

Dr Victor Strecher further gives another exercise; it's called The Headstone Test. I know it sounds a little weird. But here's what I'd like you to think about. What if you were to die today or tomorrow, what would you want on your headstone? What kind of epitaph would you want? What would you want people saying about you, about the mark that you left in this world, your legacy, the mission that you had for other people? What would you want people to say? Would you want people to say, he was the richest person? Wow, now you're the richest person in the cemetery/cremation ground. That's awesome way to go, good job. Or would you want people to say, he was so kind, he changed my life? So that's what I'd like you to think about. When you're thinking about The Headstone Test, I want you to think about the fact that you're here for this brief period of time, what kind of legacy would you want to leave?

All these things like mortality, salience, thinking about what matters most is really important to your purpose in life. So let's put this into some type of framework that makes some sense. So these are the things that matter most to me and I'm going to start reflecting on them, and that would be called self-affirmation. So for one, I want to be a family man. I care a lot about that. I want to be a truth seeker. I want to be a scientist. I also want to be a good teacher. I want to be a supporter of the arts. I want to be a visionary leader in my place of work. I want to be a friend, a good friend to the people that I know. I want to be fun-loving. So these are the things that matter most to me. There will be other things that matter most to you. All of us are different and it makes perfect sense for all of us to have a different model of these things working together. I call these things though, my be goals, because I want to be a family man. I want to be a truth seeker. I want to be a visionary leader, etc. These are central. These are my goals and these 'be' goals for my purpose in life. So this is my purpose. So, my 'be' goals form my purpose in life. You want to start living purposefully. You want to engage your best self. Remember those best-self words we were using? Being kind, being generous, being communitarian, all of those things, being eco-friendly, whatever those best-self ideas are, how do you apply your best self to your purpose? Then you become purposeful. And when you become purposeful, then you're starting to really live a big life. So the way I think about this is that self-affirmation, your reflection on what matters most in your life, leads to a purpose in your life. This is central, self-organizing life aim. And once you have a purpose, then you can apply your best self, you can engage your best self to this life purpose and become purposeful. When you have those three things going for you, I would say you're living a pretty big life no matter who you are.

So Socrates said that the unexamined life is not worth living, one of the most famous statements in all of humankind. Aristotle said, "That's right, Socrates. But you know what? The purposeless life isn't worth examining in the first place." Don't you love that two-sided coin? It's important to examine your life, but it's really important to examine your life that has purpose in it. So the two really work hand in glove to form this beautiful match, and that's what we're going to be talking about.

Socrates by the way was a Street Philosopher. He had a lot of famous students like David and Plato. So Plato was the student of Socrates, and Socrates was considered so smart, and every once in a while though on the street, remember he is a Street Philosopher, every once in a while, one of his students would ask him a question that he really had a hard time with and said, "I need to consult my inner daimon, my true self." Remember the Othman, this god-like self or true self, the Greeks had this term for that true self and was called the daimon. So every once in a while, if Socrates was stumped, he'd pop back into an alley, may be on the street, and consult this inner daimon to figure out, "What's the right answer? Twenty minutes later he may come out and say, "I know exactly what the answer is." So his students likened him interestingly to the Greek terracotta sculptures. There are all these terracotta sculptures that Greeks would make, they're beautiful. But if you tap them very often the Greek sculptures would put this little golden figurine in. The golden figurine was usually of some major gods like Zeus, and they call that little golden figurine the daimon, and they said, "You know, Socrates is just like that." Socrates may not be handsome on the outside, but inwardly he has this daimon and he's so in touch with this true god-like self, that special inner daimon, it's so cool. In fact, Plato, again the student of Socrates, and by the way, Aristotle was a student of Plato, so these guys were all contemporaneous, but you have Plato saying that keeping the well-ordered daimon that lives within us is really important. If you can do that, you will become, in his words, supremely happy. So keeping well-ordered the daimon that lives within him, he must indeed be extremely happy. So think about this word daimon. That's the root word of a word we use a lot now, the Greeks used it all the time in ancient Greece, but we use it a lot now in science, eudemonic. Eudemonic really refers to being in touch with this true self, this inner god-like self that you have.

But Aristotle also said that there are two forms of happiness. There is this eudemonic form of happiness, but also there's a hedonic form of happiness, and I'm guessing you all know what that means too. So hedonism refers to pleasure, it refers to immediate gratification. So it might refer to being super attractive or super-rich or having great prestige, or having a trophy, spouse, or having super nice car, whatever those things are that are materialistic, having hedonic happiness relates to their materialism. By the way, Aristotle wasn't totally down on hedonic happiness or well-being, he said all of us have those, all of us have both in fact, but we have different mixtures of both. So, some of us may be more eudemonically well and happy than others are. Others are very hedonically well or happy. But if all we are a hedonically happy people then, and he uses this term, then we are like grazing animals. Well, we all like to graze, we all love good food or good wine or good sex or nice car, or good vacation, a good experience. In general, all of us like pleasure. We all like, and to some extent crave some hedonic happiness. We all need to have also this eudemonic well-being, this eudemonic happiness.

Scientific study of Purpose in Life

In order to validate the purpose in life scientifically, Dr Victor Strecher explored and unpacked that just a little bit because modern scientists now have actually started looking at what's going on when you're a eudemonically happy person versus a hedonically happy person, and this is a very cool study that was done looking at a part of the brain that relates to rewards, the **ventral striatum** [3] which is getting more oxygenated blood flow, it's becoming more active. That ventral striatum is our reward center. These very clever neuroscientists said, "Well, let's find out whether some people are rewarded by some things more than other things." Really cool study. So here's what they did. While in MRI, people were asked two questions. One question was, here's some money, now how would you spend that? Think about how you might spend it on other people. So this is very focused on eudemonic well-being. Then while in MRI, they were also asked this question. Here's some money, now how might you spend it on yourself? So there'd be more hedonic. Some people it turns out, their ventral striatum really got a lot of blood flow when they're thinking about how they would spend it on other people. Whereas some other people in MRI, got more blood flow when they were thinking about how to spend it on themselves. So hope that's making sense. So they could essentially define eudemonically happy people from hedonically happy people by what their brain was doing, and what's cool here is that brains don't lie. I mean, you might lie on a survey when asked these questions, but your brain is not going to lie because your brain's reward system it's going to go off depending on what the question was and you can't control that. So it's a really cool study. Now what they also did even before they were going into MRI, these subjects completed a form to look at their depressive symptoms. So how depressed they were before going into MRI. Then they were asked these questions, and then a year later they were re-asked these depressive symptoms questions and they found an interesting outcome. They found that the eudemonically well people, the people who had more blood flow going into their ventral striatum when thinking about how they would spend money for other people a year later, they had fewer depressive symptoms. The hedonically well people had more depressive symptoms, and this wasn't a little finding, it was a very big effect. So it's very cool about this study, is that brains don't lie. Your brain is essentially telling these researchers whether you're eudemonically motivated or hedonically motivated, and it turns out that the eudemonically motivated people end up becoming healthier mentally a year later, really amazing. So let's look at this idea of eudemonic and hedonic. These are pretty odd terms, they're old Greek terms. Let's look at a more modern terminology for eudemonic and hedonic. It might be transcending or self-transcending. I'm thinking about things bigger than myself, I'm thinking about love or community or gratitude, or empathy; whereas hedonic people are thinking in a more self-enhancing way. So they're thinking more about fame and fortune and attractiveness, and things like that, so much more self-enhancing. So there's been a lot of research that use those terms, but we might be able to map both eudemonic well-being with self-transcending and hedonic well-being or purpose with self-enhancing.

So let's take a look at the idea of self-transcending values. We wanted to find out whether these self-transcending or eudemonic values produced different neural responses when we were threatening people with a health message. So we started with people who are sedentary, these were couch potatoes. They really needed to get off the couch and start working out. When you start telling a sedentary person, a couch potato, you need to get off the couch and start working out more, that's a threatening message. So we wanted to take a look at couch potatoes or sedentary people who were self-transcending, who had a lot of very strong self-transcending values versus sedentary people who had very self-enhancing values, we wanted to see the difference in responses to this threatening message, "Hey, you need to work out more." So this is what we did. We took these self-transcending versus self-enhancing people, put them into MRI, we sent them this threatening message, "Hey, you need to work out more." Here's what happened to their brain. Their amygdala, and let me explain what an amygdala is. The amygdala is a reptilian part of our brain, it's a very old, hundreds of millions of years old in our brain, and it relates to fear and aggression, very ancient part. As opposed to our ventral medial prefrontal cortex, which is very modern and superhuman, this is, we often call it the reptilian part of our brain. Here's what we found. We found that the transcending people when threatened had very little amygdala response. They had very little response related to fear or aggression in the brain. Whereas in the brain, if you had a more hedonic or self-enhancing set of core values when we threaten them that they needed to work out more, that amygdala went nuts, that amygdala had a lot more oxygenated blood flow going to it, it became very active. In other words, that fear and aggression center became super-active. So the next logical question, at least to us was, what happens when we enhance self-transcendence, and we thought we could enhance self-transcendence while they're in MRI. So while in MRI we asked sedentary people to think more about their most important transcending values versus their least important values, and sure enough, when thinking about their most important values, more blood flow went into this ventral medial prefrontal cortex, is very special part of our brain, that's really important to know. Now we did that through enhancing their core self-transcending values. But we also did it in one other way. We had them think about love and kindness, and we did it through what's called loving-kindness meditation, which is a really beautiful meditation. When we had them engage in either thinking about their core purposeful values or in a separate study, we had them thinking about love and kindness through loving-kindness meditation, we found more blood flow once again, going into this ventral medial prefrontal cortex. When you express happiness and freedom from suffering through this loving-kindness meditation; it actually improves your purpose in life.

In Indian context, ventral medial prefrontal cortex (in my childhood, I have seen the photo of Lord Shiva printed on calendar showing the third eye of Lord Shiva at the middle point of forehead exactly at the same place where Ventral medial prefrontal cortex is located) is widely made use of in Meditation which is essential part of Yoga system and is so important thing that one has made it part of one's life. It improves the physical health of brain. The brain starts working more efficiently and one starts thinking about new ideas with calmness. During meditation, the amygdala does not come into picture as it responds to fear or aggression only which is absent during the meditation state. Since meditation works on the pre-frontal cortex in the brain causing its thickness or more blood flow which in turn enhances the brain functioning i.e. increases awareness, concentration and improves decision making strength also. This is how meditation affects the functioning of brain which evolves mindset and helps in finding the purpose in life.

Philosophical Concept of Purpose in Life

Philosophical Concept of Purpose in Life

The philosophical concept of purpose in life is related to these two factors, and these two factors are related to a certain part of the brain that becomes active, and when that part of the brain becomes active, then suddenly, a lot of change happens. We're able to better organize our life, we're better able to manage and change our behaviors, which is great. We're going to start talking about existentialists' view of purpose, which is really interesting and super relevant to what we'll be talking about. Then we'll start moving toward a method of linking our behaviors to our purpose. So let's start off 500 years ago. So at that time, we were in an agrarian society, so we might have been butchers, or we might have been gardeners, or we might have been restaurateurs, we might have been pharmacists, we might have been playful as well. In fact, we were playful. If we did all of those things well, then we all got to dance, basically. We all got a chance to party and have a good time. So let's go to these three women out in the field, and let's just say that the young one talks to the older woman as they're walking out into the field to start raking the hay, and she says, "Yeah, I'm thinking about a new purpose in my life." Just assume that she wasn't happy with her current purpose. Let's say that she had heard from somebody in one of the other villages about this woman named Joan of Arc, and how awesome she was and, "I'd like to be Joan of Arc," she says. That's great. So the older woman says, "Are you crazy? Don't even think of what happened to Joan of Arc. That was horrible. You do not want to be Joan of Arc. You do not want that." Then she may say, "Well, I'm inventive. How about if I invent a new rake? Because I don't like the kind of rakes we have. I'll bet we could do a lot better with a new rake." Then the older woman says, "Look, stop this. This is crazy talk. You don't want to do this. Let me tell you a little bit about the universe here, just for a second." So as they're walking out in the field, she explains, "Look, here is the entire universe. We on Earth, this planet, are the center of this universe. We have this God, and this God tells us what our purpose is. It's as simple as that. We live in the center of the universe, God created us with a purpose, and that is it, and that's what we're supposed to do. If we obey Him, then we get to party. Life is really good if we obey Him. But if we don't, bad stuff happens. Like really bad stuff happens to us. So look at these people. These are people who thought they wanted a new purpose. This is not good for you." So basically, she goes out in the field. I love my purpose. So now, let's move just about 150 years ago. Life is very different. There is now science. There is an industrial revolution. A lot is changing. We're now starting to explore in a very new way. In fact, now we understand we're not the center of the universe. So when Nietzsche was around, 150 years ago, he understood that science was starting to take over this view that we are the center of the universe, and God had a plan for all of us. At least, that's what he believed. So he said basically, in fact, this is his quote, he said, "God is dead, and we have killed Him." What he meant by that is science has essentially killed off God. So when that happens, he was thinking about people like this in the field going, "Wow, they're going to be lost. Because if there is no meaning, if they're in this vast universe where they're just a tiny speck in the universe, they're going to have to find their own purpose." So in "Thus Spoke Zarathustra", [1] this is one of the books that Nietzsche wrote, in the beginning is this amazing metaphor. It begins with a camel. This camel says, "Load everything up on my back. Load all the joys and the sorrows and the illnesses. I want to experience everything." Once this camel is fully laden, fully educated, the camel gets metamorphosizes into a lion. The lion goes out into the wilderness and finds this dragon. On this dragon are scales, and on every scale are written the words thou shalt. Now, what does that mean? Well, this is the dragon of religion to Friedrich Nietzsche. This is the dragon of what that community in the agrarian society was saying. This is your purpose. This is the dragon of the government. This is the dragon of parents, of everybody else saying, "You will have this purpose. You shall do this. You shall act that way." The lion, remember the lion was metamorphosized from this camel who became fully educated. The lion basically looks at the dragon and says, "What do you represent?" The dragon says, "I represent the value of all things. All the values of things glitter on me." In fact, this is a really cool quote from Nietzsche in Thus Spoke Zarathustra. He said, "The values of 1,000 years glitter on those scales." So he's saying for a long time, we've had the same kinds of values, the same kind of structure. We've all been told what our purpose is. We have no choice, in other words. In Thus Spoke Zarathustra, the lion slays the dragon and then the lion metamorphosizes one last time. The lion gets metamorphosizes into a child. This is what Nietzsche says, "Innocence is the child, and forgetfulness, a new beginning, a game, a self-rolling wheel, a first movement." So what he's talking about here is how this child now doesn't have the same values that their parents had, or that society had, that religion told this child what to do. This child has completely new, fresh beginning. He gets an opportunity to create his own purpose in life. This is really relevant to modern society now, isn't it? He was saying that in the past, we are all given a purpose, but in order to find your own purpose, you need to first become educated. Once you're fully educated, you become this lion. Then this lion rejects what everybody else is telling him what to do. What Nietzsche's talking about in the innocence of a child, the forgetfulness of the old values, a new beginning with new values that this child-like person starts creating on their own, is building their own demon inside, building their own set of core values, but based on education. Remember, that camel becomes fully educated, and then the camel becomes a lion. Then the lion slays the dragon of thou shalt and says, "I am going to build my own life. I'm going to take the resume that my parents gave me and tear it up. I'm going out into the world as a new person to create my own values and my own purpose in life."

In other words, he's just become a superman. A person who creates his own values, his own purpose, and living a fully independent life, this, by the way, is the process that Carl Jung called individuation, that I am creating myself as a new fresh individual, not obeying the rules and laws or what everybody else says. Let's enter Jean-Paul Sartre. Jean-Paul Sartre actually said, "We are condemned to be free." We think that freedom is wonderful but what happens if we become truly free in that Nietzscheian type of way? It's kind of scary because suddenly we have to create our own meaning, our own purpose out of life, because we're not waiting for some other entity to do it, whether it's the government, or religion, or our parents, or society, anything. We're building our own purpose, our own meaning in this world, and we have to create our own light, as Stanley Kubrick had said. So Jean-Paul Sartre said this interesting thing. He said, "With science now, with technology, hey, everything has been figured out, except how to live." So that's what purpose is all about.

This is Albert Camus, another existentialist philosopher, a French existentialist philosopher. As the Nazis were invading Paris during World War II, he was just finishing up this amazing book, an existentialists book called "The Myth of Sisyphus" [2]. In the beginning of The Myth of Sisyphus, he was asking this philosophical question. In fact, he said it's the biggest philosophical question. Why don't we all just kill ourselves? Why don't we all just commit suicide? Life is so futile, the universe is so vast, and we're tiny specks in it. When you look at the vastness of time, we're here for the briefest of seconds; the briefest of moments, what we do doesn't really matter. Our lives are essentially futile and pointless, and if it's painful, why don't we just kill ourselves? So he asked that really difficult philosophical question. He said, "It's almost like Sisyphus every single day rolling this giant ball up a mountain, only to have that ball, that rock roll back every single night." How futile can that be? Sisyphus, as you might remember, was a Greek god who kind of pissed off all the other Greek gods so much that they said, "For eternity, Sisyphus, you're going to have to roll up this ball up this mountain every day just to have it roll back down." I can't imagine anything more futile and more horrible than that. Yet, he writes this book called The Myth of Sisyphus. So what is he talking about? He said, "You know what? When you really think about it carefully, Sisyphus's fate, no matter how futile it was, belongs to him. His rock is his thing." Now, what does he mean by his rock is his thing? What does he mean by thing? This is what he means. His thing is his purpose, and if he can find purpose out of moving that rock up this mountain no matter how silly that sounds, no matter how futile that is, then as he says, "This universe henceforth without a master seems to him neither sterile nor futile." One must imagine Sisyphus happy. These are the last words in his book, "The Myth of Sisyphus". So he starts out by saying, "Wow, life is so horrible and futile." Then at the end he goes, "Wow, if you can find meaning and purpose out of this vast universe, even if you have a small thing that you're doing, you can be happy." That's a really key factor in framing what we mean by purpose, and we'll get to that later when we talk about, for example, a custodian at NASA, where when he's approached by John F. Kennedy and John F. Kennedy says, "Hey. I'm J. Kennedy. What do you do?" He says, "Well, Mr. President, I'm helping put a man on the moon." Everybody can have a job, can have a life, can have some, can extract some kind of meaning from what they do, and are what Albert Camus was saying.

Here's a little story about Albert Camus [3] the French philosopher who really walk the walk. A lot of philosophers might be academic philosophers or other people who teach all the time or who write books. They talk about living big lives but maybe they didn't. Albert Camus is an exception, he lived an amazing life. So interesting we talked last time about the Myth of Sisyphus is a wonderful book about purpose. That's really one of the central books in existential philosophy. He wrote that while the Nazis were invading Paris. They literally were marching into Paris while he was finishing the book in Leon, France. So during that time, imagine how sad that would be if you're a French person. Well, Albert Camus joined the French resistance. Now, that is not a trivial thing to do during World War II. If you're in the French resistance and you are caught by the Nazis, they would continue to torture you until you gave up the names of your compatriots, then they would capture them and torture them till they gave up the names of their compatriots and then they would kill you. So this was not trivial to be part of the French resistance. Remember what Albert Camus was saying all along, that life is futile, that there's no meaning in the universe. Albert Camus totally bought into that, but he said, "You know what; I need to find some meaning in something no matter what rock. I'm Sisyphus and I'm pushing this rock up this mountain. Whatever futility I have in my life, I have to find something that I can find meaning from and I'll find meaning from France." He was an atheist like many existentialist philosophers were, although not everybody and we'll introduce you to an amazing existentialist philosopher who was not an atheist, but he was an atheist. He didn't believe in God, but he decided to believe in France. In believing in France he said, "Now I have a purpose in my life. Now I have a direction in my life and I am willing to live or die for that." Incredible, so in other words, what he decided to pick as his purpose was a cause. Remember when we're talking about how to find values in your life. What do you value in your life? Remember this one, what causes you care about?

So that's what Albert Camus did in his life. He picked a cause that he really cared about, a cause that he was willing to live or die for.

On the same context, Kierkegaard's [4] writes in the Journal on August 1, 1835 "The thing is to find a truth which is true for me, to find the idea for which I can live and for which I can die..." (Kierkegaard's Journal on August 1, 1835)

Further Kierkegaard's writes that "my posterity my confidant as I leave behind all these words--after I found a truth which was true for me and for which I have lived, found a mission, a destiny, a service to an idea, an idea fixe whose time had come in this dark heart of an age of transition
and gradually unfolded by stages to array my life with
the fruits of consecrated joy". (Kierkegaard's Journals, December 1849)

All the above-mentioned existentialist philosophers are unanimous on the point that everyone should have a definite purpose in life. For this you should not depend on anyone because no one will be able to help you in this regard. After the purpose is fixed, do whatever you can to work in that direction and be ready to live or die for it.

How purpose changes our life?

HOW PURPOSE CHANGES OUR LIFE?

So let's start by getting into the pathways or mechanisms of how purpose can actually change our lives. And I see three different types of pathways [1]. One would be a psychological pathway, the second would be a behavioral pathway, and the third would be a biological pathway. So we're going to get into all three.

Psychological Pathway:

We're going to start with this psychological pathway. And we're going to begin with stress or stressors. I like to use the word stressor because stress is really the experience that we might have from stressors. We're not always stressed out by stressors, but I'd like to think about it in terms of having a stressor and then the response to the stressor, which we would call stress. So let's take a look at challenges and stressors in our lives. And initially I'd like to focus on this pathway that with stressors that we might have in our lives. And those stressors could be earthquakes, it could be a tsunami, it could be the loss of a loved one. It could be an illness; it could be cancer, for example, could be COVID-19. It could be lots of different things. The idea here is that when we experience these stressors, purpose in life can buffer the negative impact of that stressor.

Now let's take a look at your brain and what's happening. So there's a really cool study looking at what happens. They put people into MRI, Magnetic Resonance Imaging [2]. They showed them images such as a dog starting to attack them. And that was designed to increase this part of the brain that we've talked about before, called the amygdala. This is our fear and aggression center, very old center, over a 100 million years old, very reptilian part of our brain. And then we have this ventral medial prefrontal cortex. This is a very human part of our brains. Primates have a lot of this. We have more than any other primate of this ventral medial prefrontal cortex. But if you're in MRI and you're having your brain scanned and suddenly an image of a rabid dog is lunging at you and attacking you, what happens almost right away, within a matter of a second or two is that, that amygdala gets more blood flow. So you end up with lots of activity in your fear and aggression center. And at the same time, your ventral medial prefrontal cortex shrinks down in activity. Just imagine this in the real-world, something's really scaring you. You freak out. And you're also not thinking very clearly because you're just too busy being scared. You get that hair-raising experience, right? If you've ever seen a horror movie or you listen to the media sometimes about horrific things, your amygdala can start flashing and it set fear and aggression center. That's kind of dominating your behavior then, and you're VmPFC or ventral medial prefrontal cortex, your decision-making isn't doing very well. It turns out for healthy people, for resilient people, that within a couple of seconds, the amygdala starts shrinking again as the VmPFC actually becomes more active. Now think about what's happening for a second. At first, you're freaked out and the amygdala is going; you're scared right now and at the same time you're not thinking. But within a couple of seconds you go, "Okay, what do I do about this? What do I do about this problem?" And that's where this ventral medial prefrontal cortex is very active and the amygdala starts shrinking down. Isn't that cool? So that's what happens among resilient people. Not everybody is resilient unfortunately. People who have been abused as children very often don't have that bounce. I love to call it a bouncer because the amygdala and the ventral medial prefrontal cortex engaged in this dance. You really need both. It's really important to have that fear center. But if the fear center keeps dominating, then you're just going to be scared all the time or aggressive all the time. Kids who have gone through emotional abuse and then start growing up very often don't have that bounce when they're scared, when they're when they're threatened with a stressor or a challenge, they just get scared or aggressive. And that's a real problem, isn't it?

So there is a study that just came out very recently, a super cool study, looking at adults and asks them how purposeful they were, how strong their purpose in life was, but then also ask them to recall whether they had any abuse as children. So of all the people who were abused as kids, we know that there's a higher level of depression overall, just on average. There's greater level of depressive symptoms among adults who were abused as children. They wanted to find out whether purpose was actually buffering this impact. So in other words, if you were abused as a child, but now as an adult have a strong purpose in your life, do you have as many depressive symptoms? So let's start by looking at the adults who cited emotional abuse as a child. And they can look at a range. It could have been mild abuse all the way to really severe abuse. And they looked at their depressive symptoms. Let's look at the adults who have a low purpose in their lives. If you have a lot of abuse, you have many more depressive symptoms. So if you have more emotional abuse and a low purpose, you have far more depressive symptoms. Let's look at the people as adults who have a high strong purpose in their lives regardless of the amount of emotional abuse, which you reported it as a child, if you're an adult with a strong purpose in your life, it doesn't impact the amount of depressive symptoms that you have. So this again is that buffering hypothesis at work, we see this as what's called a statistical interaction. So there is an interaction where purpose in life becomes a moderating factor, moderates the impact of childhood abuse on your depressive symptoms. So this is again, this buffering hypothesis related to a stressor, purpose and resilience. So a person who probably represents resilience more than anyone in my mind is Viktor Frankl who had gone through three different concentration camps. He was made the physician to prisoners in these camps because he was a physician, but he also was a prisoner himself. And he noticed that many of the prisoners would die of illness, they would die of starvation, and often they were just simply murdered outright. But he found that people who had a stronger purpose and could maintain a stronger purpose and meaning in their lives were more likely to survive if they weren't murdered outright. So this is kind of the classic case of purpose buffering the impact of extreme stressors and making people more resilient. And in fact, he wrote in

"Man's Search for Meaning", "Woe to him who saw no more sense in his life, no aim, no purpose, and therefore no point in carrying on. He was soon lost."

Sometimes these stressors can actually increase your purpose in life, or create a stronger, more authentic purpose in your life. And this new purpose in your life can create growth, and we might call that posttraumatic growth. So I'd like to cover this idea of posttraumatic growth. There are scales of this, psychological measures of posttraumatic growth, and often they relate to these kinds of questions. So these are three questions that are part of a very popular posttraumatic growth scale. And they ask subjects to report just how much they agree or disagree with these statements. I changed my priorities about what's important in life. I established a new path in my life. You notice that those two are directly related to purpose and having a strong purpose in your life. So what's important in your life, that's your core values, and values, as we know, are really part of having a purpose. I have a new path or direction in my life. This is purpose related. And then the third question I added in here, this is part of the scale as well. I discovered that I'm stronger than I thought I was. So think back to some event or some time where you were really challenged in your life. Now look back on that. Ask yourself; am I stronger now than I was before? Did that experience actually help me grow? So want to get into that and the role of purpose in life in that case. So very often these stressors cause a new direction in your life, and also improve your self-confidence or yourself efficacy, your sense of strength, and your ability to solve these kinds of problems, which leads to greater growth.

Now, look at all the things they were looking at. They looked at things like how curious are you? How optimistic do you tend to be? How integrated are you in your community? In other words, what kind of social network or social support might you have? Those weren't predictive of this increasing posttraumatic growth. What they found was that gratitude was, and also purpose in life was. These are two transcending characteristics of people. So if I can feel gratitude on a regular basis, if I have a transcending purpose in my life, those two things were predictive among these veterans over four years of growth. We can also look at illness as a predictor of purpose. Very often when we get sick, especially some major illness likes a cancer, or if we have a sudden heart attack, or some major issue, sometimes that actually can give us a purpose in life. We don't just shrivel up. Our amygdala doesn't just take over and we're scared all the time. Our amygdala might flash, and we get nervous or scared for a while. But then suddenly, we start building with our ventromedial prefrontal cortex this greater purpose and meaning in our lives, this greater direction, a way to start making stronger decisions. And as a result, we start growing.

So we've talked about pathway one being psychological, and that psychological pathway often involves our response to stressors. So when we experience a stressor, if we have a strong purpose, purpose can buffer the impact of a stressor or a challenge. Another way of thinking about this too though is that stressors can actually create a stronger, more authentic purpose in our lives.

Behavioral Pathway

Purpose though also helps us change our behaviors, and this is a really important pathway i.e. Behaviour Pathway [3]. So we know that when we have a strong purpose in life, we're more likely to engage or to change our behaviors in a positive direction. And these behaviors that I'm talking about are often health-related behaviors, so these behaviors influence health outcomes. So if I decide I'm going to quit smoking, or reduce my drinking, or work out more, or eat a better diet, or get screened for cancer or something like that. We find that purpose in life often leads to those kinds of behavior changes, which influences health outcomes in a positive way and actually helps us live longer. And now there are at least three major studies looking at longevity among people with purpose, and we know that people with a strong purpose live longer, which is awesome. And in trying to figure out just why, well, there's of course this psychological pathway, because it may buffer the impact of stressors, or it may actually lead to some post-traumatic growth, which may help us live longer. But very importantly, having a strong purpose leads to greater behavior change, which leads to health outcomes, which helps us live longer. So we're going to unpack this pathway, this behavioral pathway, a little bit more on how purpose in life leads to greater behavior change. So we know that when people tell us things like you need to eat better, you need to exercise, you need to relax, as if that doesn't make you more stressed out, or you need to quit smoking. Any of those things, people kind of harping at you to tell you something like that, we become threatened, right? And what happens when we become threatened, we've already talked about the amygdala and how that increases. Well, we also just basically become more defensive, don't we? So when people say, you really need to go on this kind of diet, you need to do this, you need to do that, often we say, maybe that's good for you or for other people, it's not good for me. I know what's right for me, whatever, so we tend to just get defensive, right? So what happens when we start thinking about our purposeful core values?

Let's go to a really cool study that Dr Victor Strecher was involved with some of his colleagues. So they started with sedentary adults. These were not college students, these are just sedentary adults. They sent out ads in the newspaper saying, if you're an adult and you don't work out a lot, we want to talk to you. So these people typically had a high body mass index, or BMI, and they tended to be couch potatoes. They tended to just kind of hang out and not work out all that much. So what we did was randomize them into two different groups in MRI. So we put them into functional magnetic resonance imaging, randomized them into one group, where they started self-affirming their core purposeful values. So remember, a big component of purpose in life are the things that you value the most, remember? So we start asking people, what are those things that you value the most, we want you to start thinking about those, while they're in MRI and we're starting to scan their brain. The other group, there was no affirmation. We did not ask them to self affirm their important core values. So they're randomized, while they're in the magnetic resonance imaging machine. Then in both groups we said, you need to work out more, and we just told them about the benefits of exercising. Basically what we did was threaten their ego, we threatened them. We said, look, this is really important for you. You're sedentary; you need to work out more. So after that then we gave them an accelerometer. And the accelerometer was just on their wrist, and we were able to monitor how much they worked out as a result of this. And we gave them a Smartphone as well. And on the Smartphone in the self-affirmation group, where we're affirming their core purposeful values, every day we talked about one of their core purposeful values and how important that was. We also taught them how to work out more, so we gave them resources. Basically advice on here's how to walk more; maybe you want to walk during the day during lunch. Maybe you want to have a walking meeting, maybe at the end of the day walking around the block, whatever those things where, we gave them advice every single day. But we also included this self affirmation of their core purposeful values. In the control condition, we gave them the how to work out more, basically, how to become less sedentary, the same resources we gave in our experimental condition. But we did not include any self-affirming message daily in the Smartphone. So the only difference between these two groups so far is that we were affirming core purposeful values initially while in magnetic resonance imaging machine, so that we could see what part of the brain was lighting up when there are affirming their core purposeful values. And then every day for a month following their steps through accelerometer, think about a fit bit or something like that, those things, they have accelerometers in them and they can monitor steps pretty accurately. So over a month we could start looking at whether people reduced their sedentary behavior. So we're looking for a line that starts dropping over time, that would be, I'm getting less sedentary, I'm working out more over time. So the first thing we wanted to find out though was when we had people affirm their core values in MRI, what part of the brain was lighting up? As you might guess, the ventral medial prefrontal cortex, the VMPFC, got much more active in the affirmation group than in the non-affirmation group. So that's something we were hoping to see, sure enough we saw that. So the VMPFC was getting much more active in the group that was affirming their core purposeful values. Now let's see what happens to their health behavior. It turns out that the group that was affirming, reduced their sedentary behavior significantly over these 30 days, compared to the group that was not affirming their core purposeful value. Remember, in both groups we're saying, you need to work out more, and we gave them a Smartphone, and everyday it gave them a how to work out more. So you might expect a little bit of reduction in sedentary activity in the non-affirm group, which is what we saw, but we found this huge difference in the affirm group. We found a big change in sedentary behavior, a big reduction. Here's the other thing that we found, we found that the more activity in this ventral medial prefrontal cortex that's lit up in Green in this scan, the more they reduced their sedentary behavior. So this is suggesting that we're finding a mechanism for what's really going on. As you're affirming more, more blood flow goes into that decision making part of your brain.

Values:

Now a big question is, are all values equally valuable? Because when we're talking about these values that people are affirming, some people might be affirming values, like I have a value of having a sports car and another person may say, I value my family or my community or love or compassion. So there are different kinds of values. Aristotle and Socrates have discussed about eudemonic values, which would be self-transcending values versus hedonic values, self-enhancing values.

There could be the value of our values. Just think about this, we may have a chocolate bar. We may be thinking about our parents. We may be thinking about a new car that we really want. We may be thinking about all sorts of things. Those are such different things. How do we somehow put all those into the same scale so that we can evaluate the values that we see all the time? Each of those things might be valuable to us. But how do we construct some sort of scale or way of thinking about all those in the same space? That's something that the VMPFC does. And so for example, I may be interested in a sports car, but I may be interested also in taking care of my family. Two totally different values, right? So want to explore how sense of purpose somehow helps me put those things, assemble those into the same space that I can evaluate both of those things simultaneously and say, you know what, overall, thinking about those two very different things, I'm going to focus more attention on my family. I'm less conflicted now, and so as a result maybe for that example, I end up making more money, or having some other positive outcome. This is Emily Falk. She's a neuro scientist and researcher from the University of Pennsylvania. She does a lot more research in neuroscience and when asked about the role of the vmPFC and this is what she said. She said that the vmPFC is taking inputs from all of these other parts of the brain and integrating them into a common value signal, this kind of common space. The function of the common value signal is to help us compare and make decisions about things that aren't inherently comparable. That's really what this vmPFC is doing, and maybe its role as we think about purpose and core values that we have that are so different. We also have found in her lab that people who have stronger purpose are less conflicted. So we're always conflicted by what kinds of values, right? And the vmPFC is helpful in evaluating different values, as I said before. But very often, we have values that conflict with one another. So at the end of the day, we might be kind of tired, we get home and we're thinking, boy, I need a drink. I need some alcoholic drink, an old fashioned, or I need a glass of wine, or something. And yet maybe our kids really need to play with us too, or maybe our spouse or partner really wants to hang out with us and talk about the day a little bit more. So we have a conflict. It turns out that if you have a strong purpose, you're less conflicted. There's a part of the brain that's really interesting that we studied among people with a strong purpose versus people with a weaker purpose, and we introduced conflict to them. We introduced among sedentary people the idea you really need to work out more and that poses a conflict in a sedentary person. Well, I'd kind of like to watch TV and eat popcorn or whatever, or I'm going to have to work out. Now, I have to figure out which one to do, right? So that introduces a conflict, and we're particularly interested in a part of the brain that relates to conflict. And this part of the brain is called the dorsal anterior cingulate cortex, or the dACC. And it turns out that if you have a weak purpose and you introduce this conflict, that more activation goes on in that dACC, this dorsal anterior cingulate cortex, than if you have a strong purpose. So what this is saying is if I have a strong purpose, I'm not so conflicted. I know just what I'm supposed to do. That's a really important part of purpose as well. It reduces conflict.

Biological Pathway:

So we've talked about two pathways that purpose can lead to positive outcomes. One is psychological, the second was behavioral, and now we're going to talk about a biological pathway. We know a little less about this biological pathway, but some of the research is really intriguing and I can't wait to share it with you. So we know, for example, that people with a strong eudemonic sense of purpose and core values, have less pro-inflammatory cell production. Let me explain. Pro-inflammatory cell production is good if we get a cut right away, because we want the skin inflaming around that cut to close up the cut. But we don't want too much pro-inflammatory cell production, it creates arthritis, it can produce heart disease, it can create kidney disease, it can even cause cancers. There's all problems with pro-inflammatory cell production, and we don't want too much of it. It turns out that people with a strong hedonic set of core values and purpose, are much more likely to produce this pro-inflammatory cell production than people with a eudemonic or self-transcending set of core values and purpose. We also know that people with a strong eudemonic core value set and purpose produce more antibodies. We really want antibody production, so if there are viruses around or whatever, having antibodies is really useful for us and we need them. So we know that people with a stronger eudemonic or self-transcending set of core values and purpose have more antibodies produced compared to people with a more hedonic or self enhancing set of core values and purpose. Now, for a really intriguing study, let's go to our chromosomes and this is just a representation of a chromosome. Our chromosomes contain our DNA, and at the ends of our chromosomes are these caps, and these caps are called telomeres. The caps are almost like the plastic caps of our shoelaces that keep our shoelaces from fraying. We know that, when those caps crack or get shorter, our shoelaces start fraying and we need new shoelaces. It turns out when our telomeres start shortening, we need new lives, and it's a problem. So we want to find ways that might enhance telomere length. There's an enzyme called telomerase, this enzyme fuels our telomeres. It's readily accessible, we can take a look at it in the blood and we can find out whether you have a high-level of telomerase fueling your telomeres or low-level. There's a fascinating study about this that was written up in this book called The Telomere Effect. The Telomere Effect was written by Elizabeth Blackburn, who is the Nobel Prize winner in medicine in 2009 for discovering the role of telomeres. The Telomere Effect, about how to maintain these ends of our chromosomes that really maintain the health of our DNA, really important. A lot of their early research was related to meditation. So one thing that Elissa Epel and Elizabeth Blackburn have done, was put people into meditation retreats. In particular, they've used loving kindness meditation; it's often called compassion meditation. You wish happiness and freedom from suffering to other people, even people that you don't like. It's an amazing meditation. We've talked previously about the importance of loving kindness meditation and how it influences guess where, the ventral medial prefrontal cortex. So some of our research run by a researcher named Kang along with Emily Fock, have studied the part of the brain that is activated as a result of this beautiful loving kindness meditation. Well, Elissa Epel and Elizabeth Blackburn, after putting people into loving kindness meditation, found that it improved people's purpose in life. The improvement in purpose in life in turn, led to an increase in telomerase, the enzyme that fuels our telomeres. So you have to ask, why. Why does purpose influence our physiology? Well, one way to think about this is to go back about 100,000 years on the savanna and think about evolutionary biology. Let's just think about a little family, a mom and her two kids living in a cave a 100,000 years ago in this small village, and then suddenly a lion walks into the village, or a saber tooth tiger walks into the village or whatever is going to walk into the village and threaten this family. What might happen at that time?

You could envision the mom saying, "You kids run. I'll take care of the saber-tooth tiger." Well, what happens to the mom? Well, of course, she gets killed and eaten. But the kids run away, and maybe the kids meet other kids and maybe they have more kids. That would be a biological answer or mechanism for why pro-social behavior, why this transcending behavior and compassionate behavior may actually lead to positive health outcomes. Having a strong transcending purpose, like I'm going to take care of my kids no matter what, May actually end up with greater reproduction and replication of that person's genes, down the road, even though that person sacrifices themselves for her children. Does that make sense? So let's go into the cave here and take a look at what's in the cave. Let's say these kids eventually go back into the cave and they start making cave paintings. Those cave paintings are about a lot of different things. First of all, they may pop their own handprints up, which is found in a lot of different cave paintings around 40,000 years ago. People just loved to put their own handprints on and multiple handprints from lots of people. So there's a connectedness that was going on. They also talked about cooperation. They also talked about learning new things. So imagine how these pro-social behaviors, such as teaching somebody how to do something, like teaching somebody how to swim or teaching somebody how to hunt, that's really important. Or maybe cooperation, as in a hunt, you would want people cooperating so that they could end up with more game, so that they could eat better, so that their genes would be reproduced more likely. Or maybe things like caring, where you're caring for somebody else. We know that these pro-social behaviors, and in other words, the self-transcending purposes that people have may be very important for continuing to move the gene pool forward over time. We know that love, caring, compassion, teaching are all positive, self-transcending purposes that people could engage in. We also know even, that having an identity is important. So maybe one person who dresses up in bunny ears in his dancing, maybe that's a certain identity. Why would identity be important? Well, I think it'd be important because you'd be able to separate one person from another person; otherwise everybody would be the same, wouldn't they? So having some identity is important. Remember going way back in this class, when Friedrich Nietzsche said, "It's important to give style to one's character, a great and rare art." We talked about Nietzsche when we are talking about the definition of what a purpose is. Definition of a purpose is related to yourself and who you are, your identity, as well as what you value. We can see that having an identity, we can see that valuing pro-social behaviors are both really important to having this strong purpose. So the aim of above discussion has been to understand psychological pathways of how purpose changes our life, behavioral pathways and biological pathways.

Source: Audio-Video and online lecture by Dr. Victor Strecher, Professor, Schools of Public Health and Medicine, University of Michigan, based on his book "Life on purpose" through Coursera Education.

How purpose works in real life?

CHAPTER SIX

HOW PURPOSE WORKS IN REAL LIFE?

We'll talk about how purpose works in the real world, in a variety of circumstances, such as college, employment and workplaces, military settings and ageing and retirement, family and communities. We'll also discuss how human beings might find meaning in their lives at various phases of their lives, in a variety of locations and situations. That's what we're going to talk about. We'll start with his theory on how purpose affects people who are still young, still maturing into adults, and often in the adolescent stage, but maturing swiftly through education or military service.

College freshmen:

So let's take a look at college freshmen, let's start with them. Let's move over time, starting in sixties. Let's take a look at two key values that college freshmen would say that's really important for me. There were two key values that I'd like to focus on. One is," I want to be very well-off financially", and the other is," I want to have a meaningful philosophy in my life." Let's take a look at how that changed among college freshmen every five years since sixties. You can see that being well off financially has surpassed around seventies, having a meaningful philosophy of life and continued to grow over time. It's seen that over time, students seem to be more focused on being financially well off and probably a little less interested in having this meaningful philosophy of life. Yet I think what this book is trying to say is that, it's really important to have a meaningful philosophy of life, to have a strong purpose in your life, and to understand how to build that purpose in your life. Because look what happens, students who kept saying, "I want to be well-off financially", well, you know what? You got what you wished for and this is what we can see now.

If you look at the average personal income since 1974 in India as per the per capita income at 1980-81 prices has also increased from Rs. 1,469 in 1974-75 to Rs. 1,635 in 1977-78 showing an annual average growth rate of 2.6 per cent during the plan period. Similarly, the per capita income at 1980-81 prices also increased from Rs 1,630 in 1980-81 to Rs 1811 in 1984-85 showing an annual average growth of 3.1 per cent during the plan period. Again the per capita income at 1980-81 prices also increased from Rs 1,841 in 1985-86 to Rs 2,157 in 1989-90 showing an annual average growth rate of 3.5 per cent during the plan period. Again the per capita income at 1980-81 prices also increased from Rs 2,243 in 1992-93 to Rs 2,761 in 1996-97 showing an annual average growth rate of 4.6 per cent during the plan period. Again the per capita income at 1993- 94 prices also increased from Rs 9,243.6 in 1997-98 to Rs 10,753.7 in 2001-02, showing an annual average growth rate of 3.5 per cent during the plan period. During Twelfth Plan period, the national income at constant prices

(2011-12) has increased from Rs 8,193,427 crore in 2012-13 to Rs 9,400,266 crore in 2014-15(A), showing the annual growth of 4.9 per cent. These are the trends of National Income and Per Capita Income during Different Periods of Planning.

Source: https (National Income during Different Plan Periods, Article shared by Natasha Kwatiah)

Has happiness increased? Not at all, in fact, happiness is decreased by a small amount. So we certainly have not increased happiness by making more money. There probably is a certain threshold of money that you need to make that will increase your happiness because you'll just have more freedom of choice. That's very important to have. But we certainly have not made our overall population in India happier as a result of this dramatic increase in personal income. This is what's happening with college students as I see it as well.

If we probe further, we can see that in the weeks, months and years ahead, India will suffer from a massive mental health crisis due to unemployment, alcohol abuse, economic hardship, domestic violence and indebtedness. While this will affect most of the population it will disproportionately affect the poor, most vulnerable and marginalized groups. Nevertheless, with the efforts of the government, efforts are being made to reduce it at any cost.

There is another burning issue of deaths caused by suicide due to various reasons. Due to which, we can notice that we are decreasing our level of purpose in our lives. We can see that worldwide, nearly one million deaths each year are caused by suicide (World Health Organization WHO, 2012a). Young people are more vulnerable to suicidal behaviors (WHO, 2012b, and c). The latest data in India (National Crime Records Bureau-NCRB, 2015) report that more than one lakh persons (1,33,623) in the country lost their lives by committing suicide during the year 2015, and around 32.8% suicide victims were youths in the age group of 18 to below 30 years and around 7% suicide victims were below 18 years. Among the specified causes, 'family problems' (307), 'Illness' (163), and 'failure in examination' (162) were the main causes of suicides among children (below 14 years of age). 'Family Problems' was the major causes of suicides which accounted for 27.6% of total suicides during 2015. 'Other Family Problems' (which refers to other than 'Marriage Related Issues') have driven 2139 and 12633 among below 18 years and 18 years to below 30 years age groups, respectively (NCRB, 2015). Srivastava (2002, as cited in Raghu, 2013) reported that majority of attempted suicide were among the young (15-29 years of age), more among males (53%) than females (47%) and from poor middle class, nuclear families. Suicidal ideation is a precursor for attempted suicide and logically it precedes suicidal acts (Beck, Kovacs, & Weissman, 1979). O'Carroll et al. (1996) defined suicidal ideation as self reported wishes, thoughts, or desire to take one's own life. Stress is a psychological variable that has been attracting the attention of psychologists for a long time and has been vastly studied in relation to depression, hopelessness, suicidal behavior and suicidal ideation. Sarafino (1994) said "stress is the condition that results when person/environment transaction leads the individual to perceive a discrepancy - whether real or not - between the demands of a situation and the resources of the person's biological, psychological or social system."

Source: International Journal of Humanities and Social Science Invention ISSN (Online): 2319 – 7722, ISSN (Print): 2319 – 7714 www.ijhssi.org ||Volume 6 Issue

9||September. 2017 || PP.21-32

Military:

So let's start with the military, a common term used for Defence Forces comprising of Army, Navy and Air Force. I am going to talk a little bit about the military. There is something which differentiates the military men with their civilian counterparts. After being out from the college, one has to explore further for finding a purpose and meaning in life; apart from all other avenues available, he chooses to join the military service also. The motto behind joining military service is not only to serve the nation but also to earn their livelihood apart from finding purpose and meaning in life. Immediately after joining they have to be trained accordingly to acquire the relevant knowledge. Learning is an ongoing and continuous process within the military. Civilians who join the Army receive months of intense training that emphasizes the fundamentals of soldiering as well as the Army's core traditions, standards, and ethics. Specialized soft skills (e.g., teamwork and problem-solving), behaviors (e.g., leadership), and values (e.g., loyalty and duty) are direct learning outcomes of the transformation from a private citizen to a soldier. This training and shaping process continues throughout service until soldiers depart the military. As such, an extensive amount of time and funds are devoted to transforming civilians into soldiers. In contrast, far fewer resources are allocated toward transitioning soldiers back to civilian life. Military service gives an opportunity to excel in all spheres of life and at same time military personnel find a better place to explore the possibilities in finding a purpose and meaning in life.

<u>**Employees and workplaces**</u>

So we're talking about how purpose can help people in the real world; in real life. We started by talking about college and the military. Experiences among younger adults and how purpose can really help them in shaping their outcomes, shaping their future is really very important. Now we're going to talk a bit about what happens when you're at work and about workplaces and purposeful workplaces, purposeful employees, you could be in an office, with maintenance, a teacher, a civil servant, a politician, an executive, a freelancer or for that matter anybody who is on job either Government or private.

I can still recollect the most horrible experience during this Covid-19 pandemic when life started losing its meaning and purpose. One can easily notice the main effects on employers, employees and workplaces. There were a lot of constraint during the period and it became very difficult to sustain the very existence. There was a fear around. Medical professionals/fraternities, police and NGO's were working round the clock to save the lives and at the same time, Government initiated several measures to help employers avoid terminations (e.g. by suspending employment contracts or reducing working hours or salaries) and enable remote working and considering the pandemic's impact on workplaces and social security contributions.

Employers have had to implement changes to workplaces to ensure that social distancing is maintained, including by adapting workstations; limiting the number of people in meeting rooms; and reinforcing cleaning measures. In addition, companies must: provide guidelines and create protocols (e.g. posters) with instructions for employees; have signs marking the mandatory distances; check employees' temperature before allowing them to enter the workplace; separate employees who are suspected to have COVID-19 or have had contact with someone who has been confirmed to have COVID-19.

Sooner, struggle was over and revival of the life put everyone on the same mode as before. People started finding purpose and meaning of life again.

Living in this very society and striving to shape the future under several difficult situations, as life makes sense within the social context, it is appropriate to know little bit of sociology. So let's start with this person who essentially is the father of modern sociology. His name is Emile Durkheim. Emile Durkheim, in the late 1800s, was noticing, as other researchers were noticing, that people in Europe, particularly in France where he was studying this were starting to commit suicide at an increasing rate. So he started looking back saying, "What's going on? What's happening? Why are we committing suicide at a much higher rate?" So he ended up doing this very deep study of suicide and wrote a book called "Suicide" [1]. Durkheim argued that suicide can be a result not only of psychological or emotional factors but of social factors as well. Durkheim reasoned that social integration, in particular, is a factor.

The more socially integrated a person is—that is, the more he or she is connected to society, possessing a feeling of general belonging and a sense that life makes sense within the social context—the less likely he or she is to commit suicide. As social integration decreases, people are more likely to commit suicide.

Durkheim's Typology of Suicide:

Durkheim developed a theoretical typology of suicide to explain the differing effects of social factors and how they might lead to suicide:

Anomic suicide is an extreme response by a person who experiences anomie, a sense of disconnection from society and a feeling of not belonging resulting from weakened social cohesion. Anomie occurs during periods of serious social, economic, or political upheaval, which result in quick and extreme changes to society and everyday life. In such circumstances, a person might feel so confused and disconnected that they choose to commit suicide.

Altruistic suicide is often a result of excessive regulation of individuals by social forces such that a person may be moved to kill themselves for the benefit of a cause or for society at large. An example is someone who commits suicide for the sake of a religious or political cause, such as the infamous Japanese Kamikaze pilots of World War II, or the hijackers that crashed the airplanes into the World Trade Center, the Pentagon, and a field in Pennsylvania in 2001. In such social circumstances, people are so strongly integrated into social expectations and society itself that they will kill themselves in an effort to achieve collective goals.

Egoistic suicide is a profound response executed by people who feel totally detached from society. Ordinarily, people are integrated into society by work roles, ties to family and community, and other social bonds. When these bonds are weakened through retirement or loss of family and friends; the likelihood of egoistic suicide increases. Elderly people, who suffer these losses most profoundly, are highly susceptible to egoistic suicide.

Fatalistic suicide occurs under conditions of extreme social regulation resulting in oppressive conditions and a denial of the self and of agency. In such a situation a person may elect to die rather than continue enduring the oppressive conditions, such as the case of suicide among prisoners.

Here's what he said toward the end of that book. He said, "He must feel himself more in solidarity with a collective existence which precedes him in time, which survives him, and which encompasses him at all points." Here's what he's saying, he's saying basically in the past in France, people were living in little villages, and in those little villages, everybody had a certain purpose. Then suddenly now they're moving into bigger cities, working in factories, and they're not feeling that sense of purpose so much. They're not feeling a sense of solidarity as much as when they are in their smaller villages. The collective existence just wasn't there. So he said, "If this occurs, he will no longer find that the only aim of his conduct in himself and understanding that he is an instrument of a purpose greater than himself. But what groups are best?" Now he's starting to ask, how do we create this collective existence now that has some type of purpose to it? He analyzes political society and says, "No, I don't think political society is going to do it for most French people, and probably not religious society now because in France, at least in the late 1800s, we're starting to lose our religion. Not even the family because we're leaving our families, we're leaving our villages to start working in major cities around France to work in these bigger factories. So our families are not a part of our collective existence quite so much anymore." Then he says, "Besides the society of faith, of family, and of politics, there is one other of which no mention has yet been made, the occupational group or corporation." Which is an odd thing for Emile Durkheim to say, because he was a socialist, and you might not have expected him to talk about corporations? He wasn't just talking about unions and corporations, he was talking about the corporation being this collective existence that you could start finding purpose and meaning from. So let's unpack that a little bit. So there's a story about a custodian at NASA in the early 1960s. NASA was being reviewed by John F. Kennedy, the president at the time. The president walks up with his entourage to the custodian and says, "Hi, I'm Jack Kennedy. What are you doing?" The custodian says, "Well, Mr. President, I'm helping put a man on the moon." I love this story because this is a story about job crafting. In a work site, more and more people need and want meaning from their work.

It can be noted that what Emile Durkheim said in 1800s about France is equally relevant for India too in present time. As on date, there is still a race among the villagers to leave their families and move to metropolitan and other smaller cities from nearby districts to far off cities to earn their livelihood. Most of them are working in a very unpleasant atmosphere in the factories and living alone or most of the time in a group in very poor hygienic conditions leading to poor health. Living in such conditions, they're not feeling that sense of purpose so much. They're not feeling a sense of solidarity as much as when they were in their smaller villages.

Retirement and Aging:

Let's talk just a little more about military service particularly military veterans. Dr. Victor Strecher says "Military veterans often have post-traumatic growth as opposed to just post traumatic stress, and that the biggest predictor of post-traumatic growth is having a strong purpose in your life. This is very important predictor. So let's talk about interventions in the real world that might help military veterans after they've gone through very often really difficult stressors in their lives. How could we help them actually enhance their purpose and enhance their post traumatic growth? There's a recent study that's really amazing and it's a randomized trial. In this case, what they did was take veterans and have half of them randomized to a loving kindness meditation. In this loving kindness meditation effort, they're engaged in compassionate thoughts, compassion around people who they love all the way through people who they really dislike, and wishing those people happiness and freedom from suffering. What they found in that group compared to the control condition is that these veterans improve their purpose in life and they also improve their post-traumatic stress. In fact, they ended up with more post-traumatic growth three months later".

Now I'd like to talk about retirement and aging as and when you retire, you may need to re-purpose your life. I mean, suddenly you may think, "I'm going to retire and do a work of own choice all the time now." It may be appreciated that this transition from military service to civilian life is not going to be so easy and comfortable despite being equipped with all the experience, knowledge and perfection in the military service.

From a learning perspective, transitioning soldiers are likely most concerned with the learning needs related to their future well-being after leaving the military service; although there is provision of pre-release course/training before retirement for all the military personnel for their better settlement in civil life. Military personnel retire at a very young age say 35-40 years of age after giving their prime of life to Defence forces. As said earlier, far fewer resources are allocated toward transitioning soldiers back to civilian life. Soldiers on retirement face identity development, moral development, and personal trajectories related to their ongoing learning throughout their life. Importantly, these learning challenges are similar to civilian challenges, yet the learning curve is particularly accelerated for transitioning military service personnel who may have never reflected on their identities, moral development, or personal trajectories while serving in the military. Thus, critical steps in learning for transitioning soldiers include developing new identities, defining morals, and outlining a career path.

After retirement, if you are doing nothing else, then you're going to start getting problems in your life. So it's really important to find some way to re-purpose your life with some type of self-transcending purpose. Simone de Beauvoir was an existential philosopher and she said this amazing thing. She wrote this book later in her life about purposeful aging. She said this, "There is only one solution if old age is not to be an absurd parody of our former life, and that is to go on pursuing ends that give our existence a meaning." It's essential that we do that. Here's what happens when people start to retire. Over time, their purpose in life starts going down. People start getting tired. They have less energy, or maybe they didn't think about how they might re-purpose their life in the first place. Maybe they had some expectations that they'd start doing certain things, but then those things start becoming less and less important to them over time. So their purpose diminishes. Here's what actually happens. This is only an average, but you know what? Nobody is average. Here's what's really happening with hundred different older people as they're aging. You see that purpose is going all over the place. For a while, a person may have a very high purpose, then maybe they get sick or something happens and they reduce their purpose. So it's bouncing all over the place. So one of the questions that we might have is, how do I build a stronger self-transcending purpose in life in this later chapter of my life? How do I make that a consistent purpose over time? This is very important. Here's what happens if you can't maintain a purpose over your life.

Dr. Victor Strecher presents a study that was done at the Rush Alzheimer's Center in Chicago, looking at people who were in this retirement phase who had a lower or higher purpose in life. It turns out that over time, people with a lower purpose in life were 2.4 times more likely to develop Alzheimer's disease than people with a high purpose in life. This is after statistically controlling for health status and cognitive deficits at time Even after all of that was statistically controlled for; they couldn't get rid of this effect. People with a strong purpose in life seemed to be more protected from Alzheimer's disease than people with a weak or low purpose in life. So in interviewing Jim Loehr, I wanted to find out what he's doing in this chapter of his life, and first of all he's not retired at all. He will work until he dies, I'm pretty certain. He talks a lot about stress and he has a really unique perspective on stress that I just love. He also has a number 1 objective of any retired person. I am pretty much convinced that our bodies were purpose-driven species. When we are without a purpose, we're pretty much designed to self-destruct. This is built in the evolutionary cycle where if you're not contributing something, then you're consuming resources that really should be devoted to someone who has a purpose to make the world better. So there may actually be a natural selection component of this? I'm convinced it is. I really believe there is, and I believe that the trigger is old man stress. That when you get out from the reach of old man stress, it means you no longer really are a productive, vital force. You have to seek stress. When we no longer seek stress, when we are just sitting idle, we enjoy eating and drinking; then you're going to check out much sooner. You're going to lose your capacity. If you don't use that brain, you're going to lose it. You want to be challenged? You have to go out and do something, or your system will take over and you'll be forced to the side line in a permanent way. Which is what a purpose does? That's exactly right.

Dr Victor Strecher further believes that, whether we call it a religious spiritual dimension, we have to have some sense that our purpose is really, really powerful for this stage in my life. There has to be a purpose and it's always evolving. So a retired person, their number 1 objective is not to retire and go to the beach, but to go out and reflect on what is this next chapter? How can I become fully engaged, seek stress again, do something that will actually turn all the lights on, make me feel like I'm actually worth something again and make sure my system goes, "I'm not going to allow this guy or this woman to checkout now. They obviously are serving a useful purpose and let's keep them here longer."? So for me, purpose is the thing that ignites all the cells. We have 50 trillion cells and they're all operating from purpose.

Aging is such a fact of life that every human being sooner or later has to deal with it. It is another matter that in the spirit of youth, no one cares for it, but at some point in life when its symptoms start to emerge or old age passing through pain and suffering is faced, people get disappointed.

S. de Beauvoir writing the book at sixty-two, in her book, "The coming of Age" [2] did indeed emphasize the powerlessness and hopelessness which accrue to older people, partly because of physical frailty but largely due to their social isolation and marginalization.

Following example will clear all your doubts regarding how to live life at the old age:

The famous philosopher Socrates of Greece reached a city while traveling. There he met an old man. Both got along quite well. Socrates took great interest in his personal life. He spoke very frankly.

Socrates expressed satisfaction and said – Your past life has been spent in a very wonderful way, but in this old age, which papads you have to roll, tell me.

The old man smiled a little - "I am sure of giving my family responsibilities to my capable sons. I do what they say, I eat what they feed and I keep on playing and laughing with my grandchildren. Children make some mistakes, even then I remain silent. I do not obstruct any of their work, but whenever they come for advice; I put all the experiences of my life in front of them, alerting them of the ill-effects of the mistake made. How much do they follow my advice; it is not my job to see this and spoil my mind. They should follow my instructions, I don't request. Even after giving advice, if they make a mistake, I do not worry, but if they come to me again, and then my door is always open for them. I again send them off with good advice." "Socrates was very pleased to hear the old man's words. He said- "You have understood very well how to live life at this age."

It is very important to take care of physical health, financial independence and mental health for a happy and long life. Keeping these things in mind, how many such examples can be seen in every corner of the world that has done such things while living a happy old age that they are astonishing. If you look back on the pages of history, you will come to know that even in old age, they have done important work and continued to live an active life till the last time. Here are some such examples, which present a picture of a hopeful old age.

Lord Buddha had attained nirvana at the age of 82 and continued to travel on foot while preaching religion for a long time. Dronacharya, despite being 100 years old, used to play a leading role in the battle and provide direct guidance. Gandhiji continued to play a leading role in the freedom struggle from 51 to 77 years and along with this he continued to compose excellent literature. Similarly, Vinoba ji also undertook padyatras in most parts of the country for the purpose of Bhoodan continuously for about 13 years in the latter part of his life. Born in England in 1901, Sir Francis Chichester traveled the world alone in a reed boat during 1966-67.

Similarly, so many philosophers, scientists, poets, litterateurs, politicians etc. remained active in their creation work till the last time and continued to give their unique services to humanity. Saints Socrates, Plato, Pythagoras, Homer, Galileo, Nicolaus Copernicus, William Wordsworth, scientist Thomas Edison to great men like Newton, Cicero, Einstein are inspiring examples of this. Socrates was engaged in a detailed interpretation of philosophy at the age of 70. Plato worked hard till the last time and died holding a pen at the age of 81. Tennyson was composing crossing the Bar at the age of 80. Robert Brown was composing some of the best poems before his death at the age of 70. There are many more such examples that set an example by leading an active life even in the latter part of life. All these inspirational examples give us the same message that if we learn to plan life properly, then we can do important and useful work with our creative power and live a life full of agility, vigor and enthusiasm.

Family and Community:

So we've talked about purpose in real life, about college, about work and workplaces, and military, about aging and retirement. Now we're going to talk about family and community. Dr Victor Strecher says that "I'm going to just forewarn you, there's very little research in this area. There's a little, but not so much. There's some new emerging research that just starting up with families, but we don't know too much about purpose and family. But one really important question that we need to answer is; how can a family create a purpose that ends up lasting for generations? To me that's such a cool question. First of all, the family is a unit. The family can have a purpose. You could talk over your dinner table, Talk with the family about what our purpose is as a family. What did we represent as a family? But really importantly, can we make that last from the current generation asking that question to the next generation with their children, and with their children. We also have to recognize the fact that there are different family members that may have very different purposes, and they may not necessarily connect with a family purpose. Allowing that person some flexibility into saying, "I might not be connected with our family purpose", that may be really important. Also family purposes may change over time especially over generations. So just thinking about that, thinking about the family as an entity, as a unit of analysis, just like a corporation could have a purpose overall that people could align to, and feel proud of. A family can certainly do that as well. I asked Jim Loehr, who works with a lot of families of future budding sports stars or among people who are not going to end up making it in sports, but their family is pushing and pushing them. I asked him how he thinks about purpose among these kids that he is working with so closely. I want you to reflect on this question. Your son or daughter is chasing something. They're chasing golf, tennis, some sport, soccer, hockey, field hockey, do you like who they are becoming as a person, as a consequence of the chase. That's the only thing that matters. You are not to be a coach. You are not to be anything but the mother or the father because that can never be replaced. Your job is to make sure that they're becoming a better, more character-driven human being because of their exposure; better able to handle the forces of life or get them out."

Regarding purpose as communities, Dr Victor Strecher asks "How about purpose-driven communities? Can a community have an overall purpose? Well, that's a really exciting concept. Even though neighborhood and structural factors are incredibly important, it's also really important to think about having a strong purpose. When they looked at people who had a strong purpose, it was associated with greater mastery of the environment. What does that mean? Well, it means that if there's a dumpster in the middle of your neighborhood, that you might be able to organize your community to figure out how to put a fence around that dumpster or get rid of that dumpster, move it elsewhere. It was also associated with increased optimism. Purpose in life was also associated with increased resilient coping. They also found the purpose in life was negatively associated with the perception of everyday discrimination. People with stronger purpose did not feel that discrimination. They also were less likely to develop depressive symptoms. So you see how purpose interacts with a difficult environment. May be making people more resilient in that difficult environment, but also very importantly, allowing people the confidence and mastery to be able to change their environment to improve it, which is even more important."

Robert F Kennedy talked about this. He said, "Even if we act to erase material poverty, there is another greater task. It is to confront the poverty of satisfaction, purpose and dignity that afflicts us all. We seem to have surrendered personal excellence and community values in the mere accumulation of material things. It does not include the beauty of our poetry or the strength of our marriages, the intelligence of our public debate or the integrity of our public officials. It measures neither our wit nor our courage, neither our wisdom nor our learning, neither our compassion nor our devotion to our country. It measures everything in short except that which makes life worthwhile."

Lastly, have a purpose. What have you been put on this earth to do? Show it, breathe it, live it! Thank you so much for being part of this writing, purpose & meaning of life. I think this will help you in Knowing Yourself in a better way to greater extent.

In the next chapter, we will see the laws of success which might further help you in turning your life happier, contented and thus paving the way for a successful life.

What are the laws of

success?

CHAPTER SEVEN

WHAT ARE THE LAWS OF SUCCESS?

In the preceding chapters, we learnt about the purpose and meaning of life. To attain success and avoid failures, one must study and practice the basic rules after recognizing the objective and meaning of life.

To achieve this goal, we must follow a set of guidelines, the bulk of which were previously stated when discussing the meaning and purpose of life. So, before we look at the laws that can lead us to success, let us first define what success is.

The state or circumstance of satisfying a certain range of expectations is known as success. It can be thought of as the polar opposite of failure. The success criteria are context-dependent and may be relative to a specific observer or belief system. In circumstances of direct rivalry, what one individual deems a success may be considered a failure by another. Similarly, different observers or participants may have varied perspectives on the degree of success or failure in a situation, thus what one person deems a success, another may consider a failure, a qualified success, or a neutral situation. Due to confusing criteria, it may also be difficult or impossible to determine if a situation fits success or failure criteria. It may also be difficult or impossible to ascertain whether a situation meets criteria for success or failure due to ambiguous or ill-defined definition of those criteria.

In several fields of life, such as biology, education, business and leadership, philosophy of science and probability, and so on, success can be expressed in a variety of ways.

Other aspects of success include good physical health, fulfilling relationships, meaningful friendships, joy in self-expression, freedom from fear, the ability to comprehend others, and self-mastery.

There are many more points of view, such as spiritual, religious, social, economic, political, and philosophical, yet everything is governed by basic principles of existence.

It's difficult and impractical to fit everything, including the above-mentioned types, into this small space. It would be best to focus on the fundamental laws that govern everything.

There are universal life laws that must be adhered to. They help us maintain a peaceful relationship with the cosmos and make our wishes come true more quickly. These universal life principles can lead you to prosperity, inner peace, and self-awareness while also assisting you in developing your sense of self.

Different classes of people, such as the rich, poor, downtrodden, and middle class, may interpret success in different ways.

Rich people such as multimillionaire capitalists, chief executives of major corporations and banks, government ministers, authors, artists, lecturers, college and university heads, and others who have amassed a large sum of money, ornaments, other valuable metals, and property may view success in terms of having a large sum of money at their disposal but are still unsatisfied and yearning for more. The accumulation of money and material belongings, as well as being of acknowledged rank in society, was one factor that distinguished nearly all of them.

What did these "successful" guys think the true meaning of life was? Their life's aim, their idea of success, was money gain, social recognition, and the fleeting pleasures of the five senses. However, the more they had, the more they desired, and the less content they were with what they had. It was never enough when they got it.

What happens if the wealthy are unsatisfied with their status in life? What happens to the poor and middle classes? Isn't money, after all, the root of all evil? Is it necessary to swear an oath of poverty in order to succeed? Do we have to accept the cliché that "ignorance is bliss" if the well-educated haven't found happiness? We see that all the time in today's environment, as to how the familiar faces of the impoverished and downtrodden, as well as the upper and lower middle classes going about their daily lives? At the poverty's extremities, they appeared to be the happiest and contented.

With the exception of urban areas, many individuals in rural areas have never seen a school during their childhood because there were few primary or secondary schools in the village, and as a result, education had not reached them, even though it was now beginning with their children. These folks were illiterate, unable to read or write. Their life came to an end with no major accomplishments that provided them with a sense of fulfillment and delight.

However, their better educated children, like other civilized people around the world, have not yet begun to climb the ladder of success in the true sense. They've begun their descent, down the basement steps of false values that lead to dissatisfaction, worry, emptiness, and frustration. They aspire to reach the pinnacle of achievement. They aspire for serenity, contentment, and pleasure. They are, however, striving in the wrong direction, toward the wrong goals - straining with enormous effort downward, away from the achievement they desire.

We've looked at the riches and poverty extremes, as well as knowledge and ignorance, industry and lassitude. Let us now examine if the classes in between, i.e. the middle class, have discovered the recipe for success. Yes, these people in the lower and middle classes had more than the impoverished and oppressed in society, who are referred to as "working class." However, it is never enough, even for those who are far more "successful" in society's standards. There are numerous competitions among individuals to obtain material items similar to those found in their neighbours' homes, such as vehicles, houses, properties, televisions, refrigerators, and washing machines, among others. Although these items have become necessities in modern living, rivalry persists. They want more the more they have. And once they get it, it is just a matter of time until they use, it simply adds to their dissatisfaction because some of their neighbours have more still.

But, on the other hand, because these middle-class, so-called working-class people did not inherit wealth, they made the most of what they had by putting in extra effort and making resolutions in this regard, and today, the majority of the world's richest people, in general, and India in particular, come from working and middle-class backgrounds.

As discussed earlier, every individual was put on this earth for a purpose! Every person was put here to become a success. Every human ought to enjoy the sweet taste of success - to find peace and happiness - to live an interesting, secure, and abundant life! And in order that all might - if willing - reap such full and abundant rewards, the Creator set in motion actual, definite Laws to produce that desired result.

In the same context, Herbert W. Armstrong (1892-1986), an American writer in his book THE SEVEN LAWS OF SUCCESS, published in 1961 by Ambassador college press, California, (a book gifted by Dr. Sohan Lal Seth, D.Phil to my father and subsequently to me which I still preserve) says that "The tragedy is that through the centuries and millenniums man has turned his back on those laws - those causes of the very success he craves! The world long ago ignored and forgot them. Today, most people do not know what they are. Most people have not followed single one of the seven basic laws."

The FIRST Law: Setting the right Goal

The point of setting the right goal is to support you in moving toward your vision. Without a clear vision, your goals might not take you where you want to go.

There's a big difference between a vision and a goal. Vision is your destination. Goals are the milestones that mark your journey. They quantify and define the steps you take along the way.

Where your vision is broad and big, goals are tangible and specific. They answer questions like "when?' and "how?" and "how much?" SMART goals are specific, measurable, attainable, relevant and time-bound.

Certainly nothing in life is more important than to know:

What is real success - and how to achieve it?

What, then, is the first law of success?

Before stating even the first law, let it be said that I am not considering here such general principles of character as honesty, patience, loyalty, courtesy, dependability, punctuality, etc., etc., except as these are automatically included in the seven rules. We may assume that one cannot become a real success without these principles of right character. But on the other hand, many are honest who have never practiced a single one of the seven laws, specifically. Many may be loyal, have patience, extend courtesy, be punctual, who are unsuccessful because they have not applied a single one of these seven definite, specific rules. Even so, each of these laws covers a vast territory.

Here, then, is the first law of success:

FIX THE RIGHT GOAL!

Not just any goal. Most of the "successful" men had goals. They drove themselves relentlessly to The SEVEN LAWS of SUCCESS accomplishment. But making money, gaining STATUS in the eyes of people, enjoying the passing pleasures of the five senses, has literally strewn the pathway of history with fears, worries, heartaches, troubled consciences, sorrows, frustrations, empty lives and death.

These things may be had and enjoyed along with true success. But they alone do not bring success. The right goal includes something more.

In other words, the very first law of success is to be able to define success! Once you have learned that success is, make that your goal in life.

Do you know that most people go on through life without any GOAL at all? In fact, most people do not know, and do not apply, a SINGLE ONE of the seven laws of success! Most people never think of having any purpose in life.

Most people have no aim – they are merely the victims of circumstance. They never planned, purposefully, to be in the job or occupation in which they find themselves today. They do not live where they do by choice that is, because they planned it that way. They have merely been buffeted around by circumstance! They have allowed themselves to drift. They have made no effort to master and control circumstances.

The first law of success is to fix the goal. Not any goal. One could set a goal in which he had little or no interest, and drift into inaction. The right goal will arouse ambition. Ambition is more than mere desire. It is desire plus incentive - determination - will to achieve the desire. The right goal will be so intensely desired it will excite vigorous and determined effort. It will fire one with incentive. There should be an overpowering purpose to life. Few have ever known such purpose. Down through centuries and millenniums thinkers and philosophers have pondered, and sought in vain to learn whether life has a real purpose. Socrates, Plato, Augustine among others, speculated and reasoned, yet important question in life remained to them a mystery – an unsolvable enigma! If one could discover such an overall purpose - a definite purpose for which humans were put on earth - If one could discover a human potential greater than mere temporary existence, one would think that purpose would be the goal that should excite dynamic ambition! But - alas! Who has ever discovered such an objective as life's aim?

What is there, after all, to live for?

<u>The Vital Second Law: EDUCATION OR PREPARATION</u>

And so, if you are to arrive at success in life, you must first set the right goal, and then comes the preparation to achieve that goal. So, the SECOND law of success, in time sequence, is EDUCATION, or preparation. Education is a lifetime process with no true beginning or ending. Education consists of experience, environment, socialization and communication. John Dewey assumed that "all genuine education comes through experience."

How can one expect to accomplish his purpose unless he acquires the know-how? One thing we need to know about life - and many do not - is that humans do not come equipped with instinct.

To this extent, the dumb animals have a certain advantage over us. They do not have to learn. They never need weary their brains with book learning. The newborn calf does not have to be taught how to walk. It starts immediately to get up on its somewhat infirm and uncertain legs. It may fall down on the first or second attempt, but in a matter of a few moments it stands, even if a little unsteady at first. It does not require a year or two not even an hour or two - - the little calf starts walking in a few minutes! It does not need to reason out any goals. It requires no textbooks, nor teaching. It instinctively knows its goal - dinner! And it knows, also instinctively, the way. On its own four legs it proceeds immediately to the first meal!

I give another example: birds build nests – by instinct. No one teaches them how. Five generations of weaver birds, isolated from nests or nest-building materials, never saw a nest. When nest-building materials were made accessible, the sixth generation, without any instruction, proceeded to build nests! They were not crows' nests or eagles' nests. They were the same kind of nests weaver birds have built since creation. They had no minds to think out, imagine, design, and construct a different kind of nest.

Of course dogs, horses, elephants, dolphins, and some other animals can be taught and trained to do certain tricks. But they cannot reason, imagine, think, plan, design and construct new and different things. They do not acquire knowledge, perceive truth from error, make decisions, and employ will to exercise self-discipline according to their own reasoned wisdom and decisions. They cannot develop Moral and Spiritual character. But humans have it not quite so easy. Humans have to learn, or be taught. Humans have to learn to walk, to talk, to eat or drink. We don't come to these basic accomplishments instinctively and immediately like the dumb animals. It may take a little more time. It may come a little harder. But we can go on to learn reading, writing, and "Arithmetic"!

Then we can go further, and learn to appreciate literature, music, Art. We can learn to think and reason, to conceive a new idea, to plan, design, construct.

We can investigate experiment, invent telescopes and learn something about outer space and far-off planets, stars, and galaxies. We invent microscopes and learn about infinitesimal particles of matter. We learn about electricity, laws of physics and chemistry. We learn to use the wheel, construct highways, and roll over ground faster than any animal. We learn to fly higher, farther and faster than any bird. We learn how to take nature apart and make it work for us. We discover and utilize nuclear energy.

But we have to LEARN - to STUDY - to be EDUCATED – to be prepared for what we propose to do.

One of the first things we need to learn is - that we need to learn! Once you have learned enough to choose a Goal, the second step toward successfully accomplishing that goal is to LEARN the way - to acquire the additional education, training, experience, to give you the know-how to achieve your goal.

Most people fail to set any definite goals. Having no specific aims, they neglect the specialized EDUCATION to make possible the attainment of their purpose.

The Basic Third Law: GOOD HEALTH

Good health is a resource to support an individual's function in wider society, rather than an end in itself. A healthful lifestyle provides the means to lead a full life with meaning and purpose.

The all-important law coming next in time order is GOOD HEALTH. We are physical beings. The mind and the body form the most wonderful physical mechanism we know. But man is made of matter. He is 16 elements of organic, chemically functioning existence. He lives by the breath of air - which is the breath of LIFE itself. If the bellows we call lungs do not keep inhaling and exhaling the oxygen-containing air, man won't live to achieve any goal. You are only one heartbeat away from death! As the lungs pump air in and out, so the heart pumps blood through an intricate system of veins and arteries. These must be supported by food and by water. And so man is just what he eats. Some of the most famous physicians and surgeons have said that 90% to 95% of all sickness and disease comes from faulty diet!

Most people are in utter ignorance of the fact that it does make a difference what we eat! Most people, and the customs of society, have followed a regimen of eating whatever tastes good to the palate. Adults are babies grown up. Observe a nine-month-old baby. Everything that comes into his hands goes to his mouth! You think adults have actually LEARNED any better than nine-month-old babies?

Of course there are other laws of health- sufficient sleep, exercise, plenty of fresh air, cleanliness and proper elimination, right thinking, clean living.

The All-important Fourth Law: DOING OR DRIVE

A person may have chosen his goal. Having it may have aroused tremendous ambition to achieve it. He may have started out educating and training himself for its accomplishment, and he may even have good health and still make little or no progress toward its realization.

After all, success is accomplishment. It is DOING. They say any old dead fish can float downstream, but it takes a live one to swim up. An inactive person will not accomplish. Accomplishment is DOING.

Hence, the fourth success-law is DRIVE!

Half-hearted effort might carry one a little way toward his goal, but it will never get him far enough to reach it. You will always find that the executive head of any growing, successful organization employs drive! He puts a constant prod on himself. He not only drives himself, he drives those under him, else they might lag, let down and stagnate. He may feel drowsy, and hate to awaken and get up in the morning. But he refuses to give in to this impulse.

As true for farmers so true for many other category of people also that to succeed, must get up early and work late, and drive him. That is one reason so many must work for others. They cannot rely on themselves - they must be driven by one of more energy and purpose. Without energy, drive, constant propulsion, a person need never expect to become truly successful.

Important as these four laws are, they are not enough. Life constantly encounters hazards, obstacles, unexpected problems or setbacks. You may be proceeding along right on schedule, when BANG! - Out of nowhere comes an unexpected complication. Some sudden circumstance arises which seems to stop you completely, or at least set you back.

The Emergency Fifth Law: RESOURCEFULNESS

Resourcefulness is about getting things done in the face of obstacles and constraints. This means approaching what's in front of you and optimizing what you have, whether you're making something new or just thinking about how to do something better.

When complications, obstacles, unexpected circumstances appear to block your path, you must be equipped with RESOURCEFULNESS to solve the problem, overcome the obstacle, and continue on your course.

To succeed, you need to cultivate the ability, and the habit, of remaining unexcited, yet leaping to action on high tension, reaching the right decision, and then acting on it!

And now one would most certainly think that these five resources should be all that is required to guarantee ultimate success.

The Important 6th Law: PERSEVERANCE

Perseverance is nothing but steady persistence in a course of action, a purpose, a state, etc., especially in spite of difficulties, obstacles, or discouragement.

In Theology, Perseverance is Continuance in a state of grace to the end, leading to eternal salvation.

Perseverance in simple words is continued effort to do or achieve something despite difficulties, failure, or opposition: the action or condition or an instance of persevering: steadfastness: the quality that allows someone to continue trying to do something even though it is difficult.

Perseverance is very important for people at any age to develop because life is full of challenges and perseverance is what helps you get through the difficulties to get to what you want.

Without perseverance, you wouldn't have finished your work, or you wouldn't have done your best work. Without perseverance, your grade in life would have suffered. Without perseverance you wouldn't have learned what you needed to learn, and that might make the next level even harder.

Hence it can be deduced that Perseverance is the key to success as more and more experts are arguing that perseverance, along with other performance values, is essential to everyone's future success.

The Overlooked SEVENTH Law: GOD

I have reserved this all-important seventh Law till last to explain. But far from being least, it is first in vital importance! I have held it till now because 1) it is the very last one that people will acknowledge and apply; and 2) being first in making possible real success, I want to state it last so it will remain stamped in the mind of the reader. When serious illness strikes, people call the doctor. It is automatic for most to rely on human professional knowledge and skill - on material drugs, medicines and knives. But finally, when the attending physician - perhaps with specialists called in collaboration - gravely shakes his head and says there is no more that medical science can do - it is now in the hands of a higher Power - then, at last people cry out desperately to the Creator God! Is it possible that the living God might be a factor in determining the success or failure of one's life? Few have thought so.

People will ignore all their lives any idea of divine guidance and help - yet if one should find himself on a foodless and waterless raft after a shipwreck in mid-ocean, it is remarkable how quickly he would begin to believe there really is a living God! In last-resort desperation most people will cry out to Him whom they have ignored, disobeyed, and set at naught all their lives. Wouldn't it seem axiomatic that, if there is a compassionate beneficent Creator standing ready and willing to give us emergency help as a last resort, it would have been more sensible to have sought His guidance and help all along? Yet some have acquired wealth, lived luxuriously, and then, suddenly losing all, turned finally to God in their economic distress. Others have committed suicide. Few, it seems, will ever rely on their Maker and life-Sustainer until they feel helpless and in desperate need. Even then the motive too often is selfish.

Yet, if we are to enjoy the good things of life – freedom from fears and worries, peace of mind, security, protection, happiness, abundant well being - the very source of their supply is the Great God! Since all comes from Him anyway, why not tap the source from the very beginning? But in our day of modern science, sophistication and vanity, it has not been fashionable to believe in a Maker.

Look again at the very first Law, as it has been listed in this deceived world, knowledge of God has found little or no place in modern education. The ALL-IMPORTANT seventh Law of Success, nevertheless, is having contact with, and the guidance and continuous help of GOD! And the person who does put this all-important seventh law last is very probably dooming his life to failure at the end. Why of First importance here. It is not merely choosing a goal - any goal. It is setting as one's life-aim the right goal.

The "successful" of this world all had goals. But their goals led to material ends. They sought happiness in vanity, pride of status, material acquisitions, physical activities and pursuits. They sought the approbation of people. But people are human, and their lives are temporary. Material objects, too, are not enduring, but wax old until consigned to disuse.

The main goals of those supposed to be successful in the world usually are two: Vanity - desire for status; and money with the material things it will buy. But happiness is not material, and money is not its source.

Oh yes, of course there were pleasures, moments of excitement, periods of enjoyment. There were occasional thrills, temporary sensations of delight. But always they were followed by periods of depression. Always a gnawing inner soul-hunger returned. This in turn drove them to seek satisfaction in the thousand-and-one events in the world's whirl of material pleasures and pastimes. Yet these never filled the void. They never satisfied the real inner hunger.

These people probably didn't realize it, but the hunger was spiritual. And spiritual hunger is never satisfied by material food!

The "successful" of this world applied six of the success laws. But they left God out of the picture, and the happiness of real success out of their lives.

It seems almost no one, today realizes, how and why, we were made? WHAT we humans are and why we are? Why should we live in ignorance of these basics of knowledge?

Two basic and vital facts are overlooked:

1) While man was made a material being, of the dust of the ground, sustained by eating material food and drinking material water, he was made also to need spiritual food, and

to drink of the "living water" of God's Spirit. Without these spiritual needs man cannot be truly and continually happy.

Nothing else really satisfies.

2) The Eternal Creator, who made us in His own likeness, is creator of ALL that is. Everything man needs to make life continuously and abundantly satisfying must come from Him.

Summarizing the purpose and meaning of life and laws of success, we have to inquire the basic question; PURPOSE to Life? Is there, after all, a Purpose to life?

If we were put here by a Creator, would He have put us here without a reason? And a Creator with Mind and Power that could have designed and produced the human mind and body could not have failed to make available for humans every tool, ingredient and facility needed to fulfill His Purpose!

Of course men cut off from God have no knowledge of that Purpose. For that knowledge is not material, but spiritual knowledge. And spiritual things cannot be seen - nor heard, felt, smelled or tasted. Spiritual knowledge can be transmitted only by revelation. And this world has rejected revelation. Men cut off from their Creator of necessity are spiritually blind and ignorant, groping in the dark. So they fail to seize the proper tools, ingredients and facilities.

This ultimate potential destiny is the only TRUE goal. It is your reason for being alive! It is the reason you were born!

Those who have worked, striven, fought their way to any other goal have been wasting their lives - living for naught! They have, in true fact, been going nowhere! And how many, since humans were first put here on earth, have really known that purpose - that one right goal of life? Very few, indeed!

The time when we need DIVINE, GUIDANCE, ENLIGHTENMENT, AND HELP, is at the very BEGINNING - at the time when a young man or woman chooses that RIGHT GOAL. Without divine guidance the wrong goal is always set.

That is why the poor people possessing the least knowledge and material goods appeared to be the happiest. Actually they were not happy. They merely were less discontented. They had not progressed as far in the WRONG DIRECTION as those who smugly and vainly supposed themselves to be their more intelligent betters!

Life has a PURPOSE. God has set in actual, inexorable motion definite LAWS to PRODUCE for man every happiness, security, and GOOD thing he desires - The way of Life that will fulfill God's purpose for our being!

What then is the PURPOSE for which we were put here? Of this, mankind has totally lost all conception. To people spiritually drunk on the false material concepts of our day, the statement of that purpose would appear strange, absurd, and impossible. It so FAR transcends anything conceived by humanity in this blinded world that the statement of it would prove too great to be grasped and accepted.

The living God has set two ways before us. One, His Way, the cause of all the good things you want here and now, plus eternal life in REAL success continuously forever. The other, the way of self-centeredness, vanity, greed, envy - the way mankind has gone, in rebellion against God and His Law the way that causes all unhappiness, suffering, evils, and ends in death. And God compels you to choose!

Yet He commands you to choose the Way that leads to REAL success. That ultimate TRUE Success is something you cannot attain to by yourself. The ingredient you lack is the GUIDANCE, the Power and Spirit of God.

You must make the decision. You must set this right GOAL. You must set your will. You must expend your full effort. You must work at overcoming, growing and developing spiritually, and sticking with it. Yet God supplies the all-important ingredient - His power, His love, His faith - His guidance

To sum up, I will say that "have Faith in HIM and HE will give you THEE the desires of thy heart."

Bibliography

Chapter 2

[1]

Evelyn Marinoff -What Is the Meaning of Life? A Guide to Living With Meaning

https://www.lifehack.org/815581/whats-the-meaning-of-life

[1] (A)

Common Sense Ethics: The Ancient Greeks Got Happiness Right: 3 Steps to Eudaimonia

https://www.commonsenseethics.com/blog/have-we-got-happiness-all-wrong-3-steps-to-eudaimonia

[2]

The Guardian: In praise of cynicism

https://www.theguardian.com/world/2013/jul/10/in-praise-of-cynicism

[3]

_Dr_. SK Sachan, Human Liberty and responsibility in Existentialism: Theistic and Atheistic Existentialism, (Notion press, Chennai, 2021)

[4]

Stanford Encyclopedia of Philosophy: Existentialism

https://plato.stanford.edu/entries/existentialism/

[5]

Ted Ideas: 4 lessons from the longest-running study on happiness https://ideas.ted.com/4-lessons-from-the-longest-running-study-on-happiness/

[6]

J Pers.: Relationships between meaning in life, social and achievement events, and positive and negative effect in daily life. https://www.ncbi.nlm.nih.gov/pubmed/

24749860

[7]

The Nobel Prize: Konrad Lorenz Biographical
https://www.nobelprize.org/prizes/medicine/1973/lorenz/biographical/

[8]

British National Health Service: Five steps to mental wellbeing https://www.nhs.uk/conditions/stress-anxiety-depression/improve-mental-wellbeing/

[9]

Darius Foroux: The Purpose of Life
https://medium.com/darius-foroux/the-purpose-of-life-is-not-happiness-its-usefulness-65064d0cdd59

[10]

The Book of Life: What Is the Meaning of Life?
https://www.theschooloflife.com/thebookoflife/the-meaning-of-life/

[11]

Dr. Paul T. P. Wong: Existential Positive Psychology
http://www.drpaulwong.com/existential-positive-psychology/

Chapter 3

[1] Audio-Video and online lecture by Dr. Victor Strecher, Professor, Schools of Public Health and Medicine, University of Michigan, based on his book "Life on purpose"* through Coursera Education.

[2] Dr. V. Strecher, Life on Purpose*: How Living for What Matters Most Changes Everything. (Harper One, 2016)

[3] Dr. Victor Strecher, TEDx-Traverse City, Talks-"Life on Purpose: How Living for What Matters Most" through you tube channel (2 years ago)

Chapter 4

[1] F. Nietzsche, Thus Spake Zarathustra (1881)

[2] A. Camus, The Myth of Sisyphus and other Essays (New York: Vintage International, 1991)

[3] A. Camus, Resistance, Rebellion, and Death, trans. Justin O'Brien, First Vintage Books Edition (New York: Random House, 1974)

[4] S. Kierkegaard, The Journals of Kierkegaard 1834-1854, trans. and Ed. Alexander Dru (Fontana: 1958), 44, from Gilleleie, August 1, 1835)

Chapter 5

[1] Audio-Video and online lecture by Dr. Victor Strecher, Professor, Schools of Public Health and Medicine, University of Michigan, based on his book "Life on purpose" through Coursera Education.

[2] Dr. Victor Strecher, TEDx- U of M- on Purpose, through you tube channel (7 Years Ago)

[3] Dr. Vic Strecher, M Public Health-Talking on Purpose through you tube channel (7 Years Ago)

Chapter 6

[1] E. Durkheim, Suicide (1897)

[2] S. de Beauvoir, The coming of Age (New York: Norton & Company, 1970)

Chapter 7

[1] Herbert W. Armstrong (1892-1986), The Seven Laws Of Success, published in 1961 by Ambassador College press, Pasadena, California, U.S.A (PP 30,32,42,48,49,50,53,56-57)